D1547804

JAMIE MAYNE

From "Plan A" To Tasmania

PLATYPUS

PUBLISHING

First published by Platypus Publishing 2023

Copyright © 2023 by Jamie Mayne

All rights reserved. No part of this publication may be reproduced, stored or transmitted in any form or by any means, electronic, mechanical, photocopying, recording, scanning, or otherwise without written permission from the publisher. It is illegal to copy this book, post it to a website, or distribute it by any other means without permission.

Jamie Mayne asserts the moral right to be identified as the author of this work.

First edition

This book was professionally typeset on Reedsy.
Find out more at reedsy.com

This book is dedicated to my dog Pepper. She was born on October 3rd, 2010, and came to live with me at 9 weeks old. We enjoyed many wonderful seasons of life together, as well as a few rollercoasters & nailbitters. Pepper was always happy to see you, well behaved, extremely delicate and patient with little kids, and in her old age, a great lover of "people food". Over our 11 years together, she grew to become my most loyal foot warmer, traveler, listener and confidant. I will love her always.

Contents

Acknowledgement

A massive thank you to Rod & Jimetta Mayne (mom & dad). You have each played a unique role in keeping me alive all these years...that is, when you weren't accidentally breaking me, or misplacing me in the middle of a road trip. Without your unconditional love & support, I would not have ever developed into the strange bird I am today. I thank you with hugs, tears, food and late night card games. Thank you for never giving up on me.

Thank you to Nick, Katie, Andrew, Amy, Annika & Nathan (my siblings & their partners in crime), for encouraging me every step along the way, and for being part of my stories. There aren't enough words to express in detail the extent of my gratitude to each and every one of you for the parts you play in the theater that is my life. Thank you for allowing me to be involved in your lives, and in the lives of your children. I treasure you all, and look forward to writing many, many more stories about all of us!

Grandma Hazel, you were never really my "grandma", you were much too cool for that. More like an inspirational aunt who helped my mother raise me. Thank you for the lifetime of support, love and wisdom. And thank you for being the best house mate I've ever had! And I cannot mention Hazel without mentioning Dale…good 'ole grandpa, whose traveler's spirit inspired so much of my life, and whose generosity knew no bounds. I hope you're keepin' Pepper & Buster company in heaven…until we meet again.

A huge acknowledgment to the rest of my extended family, as well as those who have gone on before me. I realize I come from a long line of storytellers, and I hope to pen as many of your stories as I am able to one day. Thank you for all of your shenanigans.

Thank you, Allison Bown for encouraging me to write, and for supporting my mother through the many sleepless nights I put her through over the years. And last but not least, for showing me how to use Google Docs, without which, I would surely still be struggling to get all my stories in order, and chapter 13 would have been lost forever. (wink)

And a heartfelt nod & thank you to Allison's husband Randy, for wisely advising to me: "Never let them change your voice." I'm still not sure who "they" are, but I don't think I ever even met with "them" thanks to your sound advice.

Thank you to Kris Carpenter, for your tireless work on not only this book's cover, but also my business cards. Your patience with me, excellent computer skills & creative suggestions have gone above and beyond my expectations!

To my x-husband Brian, for making some of these adventures possible, for a "never dull" 18 years together, and in the end, the most painless uncoupling I could have asked for.

Baldi's in Copperopolis miraculously had a "coffee shop" section in their restaurant space for just the right amount of time for me to treat it like an office in 2021/22. Thank you to the delightful staff there who served up coffee while I labored through writing most of this book.

A little shout out to Schnoog's Café in Sonora, where I spent many, many hours working on this book; either writing, editing, or just typing out the stories I was eavesdropping on…those stories will probably end up in my second or third book. So thank you. Your "cinnamon hazelnut coffee with a splash of heavy cream, and blueberry scones" have gotten me through some tough re-writes and more than one awkward date.

A tiny shout out to Empresso Coffee in Stockton, CA…where I worked out my final edit. I chose this place because they were "dog friendly". And even though I sat there for at least 10 hours, over the course of two days, nobody ever brought me a puppy. I'd like to speak to the management please.

And a giant group THANK YOU to the countless parade of Lake Tulloch visitors who have listened to my stories summer after summer, allowing me to self edit wisely.

To anyone I missed; Thank you, *thank you*, _THANK YOU!_ Sorry I missed putting your name into print. If you feel the need to discuss it, let's get together and create another story. OR, if there's a story you remember, that you think needs to be written and shared with the world, please don't hesitate to reach out and jog my memory! I just might like to write about it. So, yes please and thank you!

1

Timeless Inspiration

When I was little I spent plenty of each summer with my great grandmother Lura. She lived in Arizona most of the year, but would come to California to stay with my grandparents at their home on Lake Tulloch during the summer months. We were inseparable during her visits, doing everything together from snacking on the endless fruit supply, to playing cards in the house, to "swimming" in the lake. For swimming times, we would get into our swimming suits, I'd dress her up with her sun hat & life jacket, and she would float in the cove while I swam circles around her, jumped off the dock and performed my endless water tricks for her entertainment. We adored each other and I just couldn't get enough of her stories!

Once, when we were playing cards together, she asked me what I wanted to be when I grew up…without any hesitation I replied "I wanna to be just like you!" Taking a moment to pause and think; *what on earth a child of 12 might <u>imagine</u> about "who" a 91 year old woman really "is",* she inquired further. "What exactly do you mean by that?" She asked. To which I replied, "I wanna be really old and have lots of great stories!"

So that's the inspiration for this book; to tell you a handful of my stories. I sway between cringing & laughing at my life all the time, the same goes for the world around me, and I believe that most stories can eventually become funny if given enough time & therapy to heal from whatever trauma they caused.

So I invite you to join me as I weave my tales and put into words a few observations of this quirky world we have all around us, if we only took the time to notice it.

P.S.

If you're one of those people who think you can't find healing in laughter, maybe this book will change that. And if it doesn't, I'm not sorry I tried.

2

Somnambulism

Sleepwalking…it's technical term is somnambulism, but whatever you call it, I've been afflicted since I was little. It's tough to say how young for sure, but the first time I got _caught_ sleepwalking I must have been about 6 or 7.

My bedroom, like all the bedrooms in our house, was on the second floor while our kitchen was on the first floor. One night, my mother woke up due to noises coming from the kitchen below my parent's bed and elbowed my father out of a dead sleep to investigate. Living in the outskirts of Tahoe City in the 1980s, we didn't exactly fear burglars or random violence from humans, but critters such as bears, squirrels and raccoons were a constant threat. Grabbing the BB gun he kept handy, my dad crept down the stairs, (probably…no, _definitely_ in his underwear) and there I was, sitting quietly at our kitchen island, place mat down, cereal bowl in place and all the other things I might need in case breakfast would magically appear. So not only do I love breakfast as an adult, but obviously I have loved it always. To this day my mom gets a kick out of reminding me how I used to ask for my breakfast in the mornings…I'd sneak into her bedroom, and stare at her sleeping face until she showed any sign that she wasn't sleeping anymore, at which point I would blurt out "I'z hungwee!" So this night in particular, I guess I got so hungry in my sleep that I didn't wait for the luxury of awareness or daylight.

Dad must have noticed that I was a "little off". So after stowing his BB gun, he made his way quietly to my side, realizing that I was completely unaware of his presence, and concluded that he'd better bring in the "big guns", aka mom. Next he retreated back upstairs to fetch my mother, who scooped me up and put me back to bed. Little did they know they were just on the brink of learning all about sleepwalking children.

The next time I got busted was when I was 8 or so. My mom recalls trying to calm me down while I was completely flipping out, physically fighting her and babbling incoherently. Mom responded to my word salad with: "Jamie! Jamie! It's MOM!" At which point I calmed down, looked her directly in the eye and said "Mommy?...(dramatic pause) *YOU'RE A SPIDER!!!!*" I don't know how she finally got me to calm down enough to put me back to bed, but after that experience, she quit trying to wake me up during a nocturnal expedition.

When I was 11, my mom was away on a retreat and I had a sleepwalking event when my dad was home alone with us kids. We were ages 13, 11, 6 & 4, and I'm still shocked that mom was brave enough to leave us with dad for a whole weekend with no other adult supervision. I had some pretty severe maternal separation anxiety until I was about 15, so mom leaving for the weekend always had a dramatic effect on me...that is, until mom was actually *gone* and *DAD* was in charge! Back then, mom didn't leave by herself all that often, so dad really didn't have that much practice with the day to day details of proper child care. Therefore, he wasn't the world's most trained babysitter…I remember having to teach him how to change my little brother's diaper for the first time when I was six years old. None of us kids seemed to mind though, because dad was _FUN_! Rod, Mr. HappyFunTime always kept us busy when mom was away. He may have ditched us most weekends during hunting season, but when dad was around, and _especially_ when mom was gone, we always had a blast. It was also the 80s in the Sierra Nevada Mountains, so while safety may have come in last place, my childhood experiences with my father were memorable to say the least.

Mr. HappyFunTime also didn't know how to feed growing humans "the right way", so our meals were all things we _really_ wanted to eat and probably shouldn't be. Our typical options for mealtimes were as follows:

1. Cold cereal. (With as much sugar as we wanted.)
2. Hot dogs. (Cooking optional.)
3. Spam. (But ONLY if dad was available to cook it properly…to a crispy death that is.)
4. Breakfast burritos. (If dad was also hungry.)
5. Popcorn. (Movie or breakfast, didn't really matter.)
6. Ice cream. (This was the _only_ item on the menu absolutely out of the question for breakfast.)
7. ANY snack or fruit. (And yes, dad counted fruit flavored snacks as "fruit".)
8. Pancakes. (If dad was feeling fancy.)
9. And finally; WhateverElseWeCouldFindInTheFridge.

These were our options. For just about _any_ meal. And we took full advantage of this agreeable situation. As an adult, I've taken care of my nieces and nephews enough to know that dad was taking the easy way out. (The fight over getting kids to eat actual food at mealtimes is _real_.) So, Mr. HappyFunTime obviously didn't like confrontation. Particularly with kids. And _especially_ the unpredictable sleepwalking variety...bringing us back to the subject at hand, sleepwalking Jamie. He also either didn't know, or didn't remember that you aren't supposed to wake up a sleepwalker. Therefore, when I had this particular experience with dad, I was rudely jolted awake when my foot hit the icy water of the toilet. Thankfully it was a clean toilet, but I was NOT amused. Dad later informed me that this is how he woke _himself_ up from "sleepwalking" when he was a kid...not exactly sure how that works from a scientific standpoint, "lucid sleepwalking" isn't anything I've ever heard of, but hey, I believe my dad, he never lies and anything is possible.

When I was 13 we went to visit mom's best friend and her family in Colorado when I fell ill...that brought my sleepwalking to a whole new level. None of that innocent, "yelling that mom is a spider" or "setting myself up for breakfast at 3:00 in the morning" stuff. This time I was determined to escape the house. After several nights of mom diverting my breakout attempts, my poor exhausted mother decided to sleep in front of the door to the bedroom where I was sleeping; that way she might get a little rest before getting tripped over by her sleepwalking teenager. The last night I tried to go AWOL, she woke up and I was fighting her for my liberation from house-arrest. At the end of her rope, not knowing what else to do, she boldly stated; "Jamie! You have got to fight this!" At which point, I started muttering, then shouting in some sort of mysterious gibberish, then went back to bed and didn't sleepwalk again for almost an entire decade.

Sleepwalking as a child I have more of a framework for what happened before I woke up; since these stories are compiled mostly from the bits and pieces I've been told by my parents who most often caught me. The events from my adulthood sleepwalking are much more surreal, since I have no clue what happened before I woke up in a strange place, thinking; *"Thank God I was wearing clothes!"*

In my early 20s my boyfriend Brian and I were visiting some friends of ours in New York City. Being young, fun & a little broke, we chose to stay in a youth hostel for the first time. We weren't all _that_ broke, so we opted for a private room. This particular "hostel" in Manhattan used to be some version of a hotel, so we had a shared bathroom, and a make-shift "kitchen" awkwardly thrown together in our bedroom space. I'm still not sure what the requirements are to call a non-traditional, rented sleeping place a "hostel". I still think they all just make it up as they go, and so long as they can keep their inhabitants rotating through fast enough to never get sued, and keep the cash flowing, who cares right? That being said, I have since _lived_ in Manhattan and I've never been able to find this place again.

On our second night I woke up outside the door in the hallway trying to "unlock" the door to our room with a couple of metal hair clips. You never really start to panic until _fully_ awake, and when I did, I started banging on the bedroom door with my palm, then my fist, trying to wake up Brian! I tried and tried, until I finally noticed the number on the door. It was 205. We were in 305. I immediately froze, fearful that a less than friendly stranger might open the door I'd been fighting to open! I then dashed up the stairs to find our door wide open, Brian passed out, no clue I was missing. I crawled back into bed and fell asleep thinking; *"Thank God I was wearing clothes."*

The last time was when I was 31 years old. Brian and I (now married) were visiting a friend of ours in Chicago. She had a lovely apartment on the 8th floor of a high rise, complete with a charming, professional doorman named Eddy.

After a very full day of eating, drinking and being tourists with our friend, we needed to take her 90 lb black labrador out for his walk. Taking the elevator up to her floor, we decided to make our descent back down with the dog via the back stairs. I'd never lived in a place with a dog where an elevator is even an option, but I imagine it's probably good to keep the dog moving towards an exit after he's been cooped up all day long…I mean, I knew a guy once who admitted to peeing in an elevator out of desperation, and I can only imagine that a dog doing the same would draw unwanted attention, plus unnecessary clean up by some disgusted housekeeper.

The dog walk was the perfect end to a very long day, so we decided to call it an early-ish night at around 11:00 pm. (As career restaurant slaves, going to actual "sleep" anytime before last call was luxurious.) I drifted easily into sleep, only to wake up around 3:00 am in the basement. It was one of those high rises that has more than one tower, but only one huge, slightly haunted feeling basement space. I remember wandering through the maze of hallways, finding the laundry room, the storage lockers, and a few other doors that were locked. I finally made my way up to where I had seen Eddy the doorman before, but his post was vacant. Apparently the place goes without him in the wee hours when one might need him the most. I couldn't go outside to use the buzzer for fear of being locked out, and didn't remember her exact apartment number anyways. The elevator wasn't an option, as one needed a key card to make it work...so, after making my way back to the basement and regaining a bit of clarity, I located the back stairway and started my hike back up to the 8th floor, where I had once again, left the door wide open.

My friend's bedroom door was shut, Brian still fast asleep right where I had left him in the guest room, and the dog was out cold. Incredibly grateful that I was not only back in bed, but I also hadn't allowed the dog to break free, I began to silently rehearse what I might have said to my friend if I'd let her dog loose. The narrative went something like this: *"I'm so sorry, but I seem to have lost your dog while I went on a tour of your basement in my sleep. But at least I was wearing clothes!"*

3

Tazzy: Get Ready!

When traveling, I tend to visit additional random and some-times exotic places simply because I'm already "so close." Much to the frustration of my first husband Brian, sticking to an original itinerary, or "plan A" has never really been a priority for me. That's how we ended up in Tasmania in 2009.

We were both approaching our 30s, and had hit a crossroads of sorts where we wanted to do grown up things like buy a house, get a dog & start a business. So we decided to flush out some travel bugs first. We sublet our apartment in New York, found someone to board our chinchilla, quit our jobs and peaced out to Australia for 3 months.

Almost right away we found a travel buddy by accident. We met Juliana at the airport when our flight from JFK Airport to Los Angeles was canceled on our way to Sydney. Juliana was in line ahead of us at the bag drop when we all got the news about the canceled flight…almost immediately, she spun around, all spunky, positive & _totally_ Canadian, then declared to us; "Hi! I'm Juliana, looks like we'll be here for a while. Let's be friends." And just like that, we've been friends ever since. Juliana was on her way to Australia for a full year. She and her fiancé at the time, decided it would be fun to spend a year on opposite sides of the world and keep up the long distance relationship. So she had gotten herself a visa, secured a job and a 1 year rental property overlooking Bondi Beach, which is located on the outskirts of the Sydney suburbs.

Our flight was delayed a full 24 hours, so all the passengers booked on our plane were suddenly hotel bound for the night. After being shuttled from the airport to the hotel like a bunch of cattle, we got checked in, dumped our stuff in our rooms, then met up in the bar for a mediocre buffet dinner, which was provided by the airline for our herd of displaced humans.

Over this pathetic excuse for an evening meal, we told Juliana that after acclimating ourselves in Sydney for a week or so, we were heading to Tasmania "first thing". I mean, since we were going to be landing in Sydney, driving to Melbourne and Tasmania was, "so close", how could we skip it? I don't remember who asked who, but we agreed to travel as a team for a while...because, while we were all English speaking tourists, going to an English speaking country, we were still going to be in a very foreign place quite soon.

After an evening of enthusiastic, alcohol inspired, ill-informed planning, dreaming & scheming, we retired to our respective rooms to await our plane. The flight itself the next morning was uneventful, mostly due to the ambien we had gotten our hands on. So when we arrived, not feeling any sort of jet-lag whatsoever, Brian and I were quite anxious to experience everything!

After checking into our hostel in a neighborhood called "Kings Cross" that morning, Brian rolled his eyes out loud when I insisted on visiting the Sydney Zoo. I was mostly wanting to educate myself as best I could about all the things that might try and kill us during our 3 month visit. And trust me, *everything* in Australia *IS* trying to kill you.

I've suffered from acute arachnophobia ever since I can remember; therefore, spiders were at the top of my personal list of critters I was concerned about, so I was off to the insect ward first. It quickly became clear to me that the creepiest ones on display in the zoo were the Huntsman Spiders. Now, while these particular monsters are non-toxic, aren't aggressive towards humans and therefore can't kill you, they *are* known for their speed and hunting abilities. Plus, with a 10"-13" leg span, and 1" body length, huntsman spiders are some of the largest on the continent. And these massive creepers don't weave webs like your average spider...instead they patiently lay in wait for an innocent meal to cruise by and then attack! They have been known to chow down on whatever they can overpower, usually other bugs, but sometimes small rodents; and that alone is enough to make me want to keep my distance. I left the insect ward that afternoon with a whole new respect for more than one species of the creepy-crawly world.

We then proceeded to explore the rest of the zoo; relearned the differences between alligators & crocodiles. No reason really, they're both trying to kill you, and there is no real reason to know the difference since you'll never find them both in the same place at the same time.

We began to understand just how snuggly koalas can be in captivity vs. when they're in the wild and either sleep all day or drunkenly fling their poop at whoever dares to disturb their slumber. I also found out that there are only a few states in Australia where you can legally hold them, and from that day on, I was determined to visit one of those states and find a koala to hold. (For the record, I _did_ get to hold 2 koalas during our 3 month stay, and I have yet to unpack those stories.)

After that we learned that you should never approach a wild kangaroo, since, while not actively trying to kill you, they're so strong and prone to playful fighting, that they just might cause dramatic injuries by accident.

Next up, wombats claimed a portion of my heart upon first sight. Having grown up with chinchillas, and having one back home, I'm a sucker for an unusual rodent, especially when they're a little on the ugly side...and those little fluff balls are just so adorable & funky with a generous side of stupid, how could I not fall in love? We picked up a stuffed animal wombat, named him "Wobby" and he became our mascot for not only the remainder of the trip, but for the next 9 years.

Finally we found the echidnas; I'm still trying to wrap my head around those little weirdos! In case you've never heard of them before, there's a reason for that...they're an almost extinct, egg laying, spiny anteater of sorts weighing around 18 lbs and closely closely related to the platypus. I seriously think God was having an "off day" when he decided on their details...either that or he put the stupidest angel in charge of making them out of whatever spare parts He had lying around on the last day of making critters.

Brian, losing patience with my fascination, completely disenchanted with any zoo, and nature in general, was thrilled when I suggested we cut our excursion short and find a bar.

The next day we started the supposedly simple task of finding a long term rental car. It took longer than we expected to secure the vehicle. Like, a week longer. During which time Juliana (or "Jules" as we started calling her) got set up in her one year rental on charming little Bondi Beach, while Brian and I extended our stay at the hostel we had booked in what turned out to be party central. We were 27 & 30 at the time, while most of the hostel inhabitants were between 18 & 23, but we kept up with those party-animals as best we could, and were pretty wiped out by the time we worked out the car.

We had planned on *renting* a car, but came to learn it was much more popular and cost effective to simply buy one. At the time there were companies that would sell you a senior car along with paperwork saying they would buy it back from you within the year at no less than 40% if it was kept in "good enough" shape. We hadn't exactly *planned* on buying a car, but there we were, buying a car; a navy blue,1997 Ford Falcon we decided to call Camilla. And this would prove to be just the tip of the iceberg when it came to things we hadn't exactly planned on doing.

4

Tazzy: Get Set!

Just a few days later, we fetched Jules from her cottage at the beach and hit the road early in the morning with every intention of getting from Sydney to Melbourne in a single day, catching the ferry to Tasmania, checking into a generic hostel and starting our exciting exploration of this mysterious island! This was long before any of us had smartphones to tell us how long things would actually take, or what to expect…so we were like the blind leading the stupid, in a foreign country, driving on the wrong side of the road.

We set out to drive the "coastal road" not realizing that this particular stretch wasn't actually ON the coast. I had become accustomed to "coastal roads" in the states where one might actually see vast ocean views along the way; we learned later that there are coastal roads like that, but this is not one of them. In reality, it reminded me more of Vermont or Connecticut, but with more kangaroos.

That first day was a little rough for both Brian and myself. I was sitting in the passenger seat located on the left side of the car, where, in the US, I would usually expect to have a steering wheel in front of me along with some sort of control of the car. And Brian, ever the control freak, would be lying if he denied having an easy go of it driving on his weird side.

Living in San Francisco, and then Manhattan, we had both been car-free for the past 8 years. So, he was not only trying to remember how to drive in general, but also learning the opposite side of the road along with a few different rules, while probably nursing a wicked hangover. And it didn't help that I was trying to give him driving directions using an actual paper map, thus resulting in our usual high tension, very quiet fighting that most innocent bystanders might not notice.

As usual, we successfully kept our drama quietly between us…so as we drove along this ruggedly beautiful countryside in distress, Juliana was content as could be, sitting in the back seat, snapping pictures left and right, completely oblivious to our private war & turmoil.

It started getting dark, and by 8:00 pm, we hadn't seen a single sign of civilization for roughly 2 hours…not even oncoming headlights, and we were running out of gas.

Now, running out of gas in the dark, in a foreign country wasn't something we were interested in, so when we finally drove through what looked like it might be considered a "town" we stopped at the only place where we saw some lights on…a "pub" where we sought guidance for a source of fuel. I ran in to seek advice and met Todd. As it turned out, Todd was the owner/employee/chef of the "restaurant"/bar/inn/general store. He informed me that if we drove for another 15 "clicks"(that's kilometers in Australian) we would see a gas station. No actual human would be on duty after dark, but the credit card function _should_ be working and we could simply get our gas all alone in the dark and hope the tanks were full. Now *that* answer prompted my next question: "Have you got any rooms?"

There were exactly two other people patronizing the pub that evening; they were a charming British couple on a similar journey as ours, minus a Canadian sidekick. So there we were... 2 Brits, 1 Canadian and 2 New Yorkers. I may have let it slip that I was actually born & raised in California, adding yet another unique layer to our part in this entourage.

Fearlessly prompted by Todd, we entertained ourselves all evening by poking fun at each other and our respective places of origin.

When Todd decided to "close" at 10:00 pm, we purchased bottles from the bottle shop (which Todd had to open for us, then close it again to go back and close the bar.) Todd decided to join us, so then all 6 of us simply relocated to the upper deck of the pub where the laughter continued with our various road snacks spread out for all to share.

Upon breaking out the snacks of chips, cheese and kangaroo salami, it was discovered that one of our new British friends was a vegetarian. Todd, having never met an actual vegetarian before, had ALL the questions, then all the jokes, and we ended up making fun of this poor guy's lifestyle choice for what felt like hours! He, being a good sport about it, decided to join us in making fun of himself...I mean, who goes to visit a place like Australia and doesn't eat meat?

Starting to feel the strain of the day, and our insides sore from laughter, we retired to our rooms, hoping that the next day would finally land us closer to our goal. Tasmania.

The next morning, heads throbbing and sides still aching, we bid our new found friends goodbye. Todd asked us to send him a postcard...when I asked him to write down the address, he just laughed at me, insisting that if we were to simply write:

Todd
  Cann River Hotel
  Cann River, Vic.
  Australia

They'd get to him for sure. Yes, we sent him postcards. And no, we have no idea if he ever received them.

Picking up where we left off the night before, we made it to Melbourne with plenty of time to "catch the ferry". As it turned out it's not *quite* that simple, since Tasmania is a bit further away than we all thought...like, 350 miles further. And the ferries are not only expensive, but booked out weeks in advance. By this time we were all so determined to get there that we might have swam! So we did the next best thing, which was to fly. We checked into a mediocre hostel in Melbourne for a few days while we planned our next steps, including reserving a rental car for our week on the island, booking a decent hostel in Hobart and deciding on a safe place to park Camilla for the week. Our flight was booked for a few days later, and then instead of doing much in the way of research, we decided to goof around in Melbourne, got caught up in life at the hostel with all the traveling juveniles, and "research" the old fashioned way! That is; listening to whatever fun gossip and exciting stories we could draw out of the various people we encountered who had actually *been* to Tazzy and come away with good reports...which of course left us excited to visit Tasmania, but completely unprepared. We *did* however learn that Melbourne is pronounced "MEL-bun" and one never says Tasmania, everyone simply says "Tazzy". I had watched "Crocodile Dundee" at least a hundred times growing up, and had never heard either of those things, so I was grateful for these important pointers.

A few days later, at the airport waiting for our flight, we met a fella who decided it would be important to _warn_ us about Tasmania and of it's inhabitants. He gruffly informed us that Tazzy is like the trashy southern trailer park of Australia. And that Tasmanians are poked fun at for being inbred thieves, uneducated and sometimes even have 6 toes.

Given all of these dramatically different and opposing points of view & opinions, I was curious to see what Tasmania might actually mean for us.

5

Tazzy: GO!

We finally arrived safely in Hobart, and after all of the stories, warnings, and general gossip, _nobody_ thought to tell us that they have the nerve to include a Labor Day Weekend in their calendar, and we stepped in it.

Similar to in the United States, Labor Day simply meant that more places would be closed, and anyone being made to work that weekend wouldn't be happy about it. Doing our best to make the most of things, we checked into our hostel, then hit up a library to see what was actually open during this holiday weekend.

The library was complete with a free Internet cafe, but right after we ordered our food and began our research, the fire alarm went off! Now, participating in a Tasmanian fire drill wasn't on my bucket list, but it would have been if I knew how much fun it would be! We wound our way through the bowels of the library, places we would never have wandered into on our own; then, once outside, made small talk with the others forced into sudden evacuation and learned much more about the island of Tasmania & the city of Hobart than the internet could have provided at the time. The island was complete with a brewery, animal rescue center, distillery, various secret hiking spots and farmers markets.

After gaining access back into the library our food arrived and we wrapped up our research, which was mostly just confirming what we learned during the fire drill. The farmers market was that day, so that would obviously be our first stop. We were all self-proclaimed foodies at the time, so finding new spices, spirits and cheeses was usually a highlight for us. Brian found some funky spirits & beer, while Juliana found some mysterious spices and local trinkets. I'd been working in cheese for most of my professional career at that point, so I was thrilled to find some new cheeses! There is a famous creamery on King Island which is an isle situated between the mainland of Australia and Tasmania. Their washed rind and the triple cream were easy to choose since they were the most interesting to me and _completely_ unavailable back home since they never make it out of the country. It took me forever to choose a blue, since there were at least 6 of them that I wanted to try, but with Brian and Jules losing patience with my indecision, I finally settled on a cute little number and called it a day.

The next morning we picked up the rental car we had to practically sell our molars for, and began our exploration of "Tazzy". I don't recall exactly what make, model and year the car was, but it was a pathetic shade of beige, had definitely been there since the early '90s, and reeked of cigarette smoke, aftershave & cheap air freshener.

Once on the road, we quickly learned that driving in Tasmania would essentially be a game of "dodge that roadkill, and try not to make any more of it." Another fun Tasmanian game is trying not to get pulled over for speeding, or "reckless driving" while dodging roadkill. We lost that game when we got our first ticket.

The first place we visited that day was a wildlife sanctuary. And after what we witnessed on the drive, we didn't even need to ask what happened to their roadkill mamas. We got to see a baby wombat being bottle fed up close, watch the baby Tasmanian devils fight each other over what seemed like garbage meat, and even hand fed some kangaroos! Feeding the big "roos" was intimidating at first since I was 5'4" and 135 lbs at the time...therefore just about eye to eye with most of them, and the bigger ones outweighed me for sure. My uneasiness subsided when I started to think of them more like overgrown versions of my chinchilla back home...throwing their heads back in ecstasy, leaning in for more chest scratches, just about toppling me over and then begging for more treats with their gigantic eyes and batting their eyelashes like drunken prom dates. I later learned that the kangaroos we fed were technically outside the sanctuary, and quite wild. But we somehow walked away unscathed, and delighted to have accidentally had such a potentially dangerous encounter.

That night we checked into the cleanest and emptiest hostel I'd ever seen. The lady at the "front desk" (which is little more than a closet) asked about our time in Tazzy, and we weren't shy about telling her all about our discoveries! From the cheese, to the special spices, to the wildlife sanctuary and even bragged about our plans for the sunrise adventure we had planned for the very next morning. Maybe it was the late hour, but I'm pretty sure she was annoyed at our enthusiasm. She was as bitter as a dwarf working in a year round Christmas shop, twice as cranky and obviously irritated at our late check-in. We opted for the budget-friendly bunk room, where she checked us in & out at the same time since we were leaving at an ungodly hour the next morning and beds would almost be pointless. I noticed during this exchange that all around the common area/checkin/game room there were decorative bowls containing beautiful seashells with crusty carcasses of huntsman spiders nestled into the spaces between them. I've had an adoration for seashells for as long as I can remember, along with severe arachnophobia, therefore, I cringed and became nauseous at the mere sight of something I love being forced to snuggle up next to something that petrifies me…I tried not to think too much about it. "Only one night Jamie, (I kept telling myself) only one night".

That evening, ignoring the choice in creepy exoskeleton decor, and regaining a bit of my appetite back, we devoured the blue cheese! Something about it was familiar to me. Like, *really* familiar. I dug the wrapper out of the garbage, and upon re-inspecting the label, I concluded that it was the "Roaring 40's" Blue, a cheese I've been serving in various restaurant settings for the past 5 years! So I just traveled to the other side of the globe only to accidentally find an old friend. *"That's fine"* I thought to myself; *"I've still got the other two, and I know I haven't had them before."* But, we'd consumed enough cheese for one evening, and it was time to play some pool before trying to get a little sleep; since the next adventure on our list was to witness the sunrise over Wineglass Bay. We'd been told it's quite the spectacle, and as someone in Hobart stated; "One simply can't visit Tazzy without seeing a sunrise!" I guess we all suffer from a bit of FOMO, (Fear Of Missing Out) so when someone says "you can't miss this one thing" *of course* we wouldn't dream of passing it up. If you've never traveled with this mentality, I strongly suggest you try it out. At least once.

We had planned to leave the hostel around 5:00 am to see the sunrise from a cliff on the east coast, so when our alarms went off at oh-dark-thirty, Jules and I sprang from our bunks practically bursting with excitement, while Brian groaned, and may or may not have cursed the day before hitting the snooze button.

Jules and I hit the ladies shower room, leaving Brian to snooze a little longer and then start loading up the car. Still a little out of it from sleep deprivation, I had grabbed the key to the room, forgetting that there was only one. Emerging from the shower room, we discovered a *very* cranky Brian. Now, as you may have guessed from his reaction to the alarm, Brian isn't a morning person to begin with and has a short fuse before noon...so being locked out of the bunk room where *he* left the car key, and with nobody at the front desk at that hour, he was left to sit, stew and get all the crankier.

Making an effort not to fight in front of our relatively new friend, I did what I always did and simply avoided the conflict. I walked to the kitchen to pack up the fridge stuff all by myself only to discover that someone had taken *one* of my remaining cheeses! I. Was. *Livid!* The fridge had been empty the night before except for our things, so I didn't think to label them as I normally would when sharing a refrigerator with strangers. There was no doubt in my mind that it was the cranky lady from the front desk; punishing us for having the nerve to be so happy around her! Now it was *my turn* to be cranky, only the object of my bad mood was nowhere to be seen and confronted...not that I would have.

We finished packing the car together, me in my bare feet. I took a minute to chill out and mourn the loss of my cheese while Brian and Jules went to the kitchen to make their tea for the road. Brian was still cranky, we were still sort of fighting in our own way, on top of that drama I was now angry at someone I will never see again, I had no idea how Jules was feeling and I didn't care.

Suddenly Brian said "don't look over here!"

Of course I looked up immediately.

And there, blending in perfectly with the fuzzy gray carpet, where I had just been running around with my naked feet, was the biggest spider I had ever seen! It was a _huntsman_. When I saw these monsters at the zoo in Sydney, I had hoped to never encounter one in the wild…I shrieked and flew onto the nearby table begging someone to bring me my shoes!! Ignoring my desperate plea, but still trying to fix the problem, Brian grabbed a bowl from the kitchen to cover the beast. When he approached, the gargantuan arachnid went from it's restful "flat" shape to it's defensive "tall" shape. Fully absorbing the horror of it all, I looked around the room and noticed that this creeper was not alone. There were dozens of them spread out all around the room, and while Brian was trying to cage them, Juliana was down on her knees taking close up photos of their creepy faces.

Finally accepting that there weren't enough containers in all of Tasmania to capture them, we decided that it was time to just go. Ditch the tea and _GO!_ After having my shoes tossed at me, I bolted for the door, the tag from my vest tickled me on the back of my neck, feeling like a spider, pushing me almost to tears! This was going to be a _very_ long day.

On the road, we haphazardly explained to Jules that Brian wasn't actually afraid of spiders at all…like, _at all_. Once, I had found a spider in our apartment in San Francisco, and instead of killing it, he simply scooped it up with his bare hands and gently placed it outside. We weren't big on holding hands to begin with, but we didn't hold hands for weeks after that.

The walk from the car to the lookout was full of nature, and at that hour, spiderwebs criss-crossed the path. Huntsman don't weave webs, but facts like that don't matter with spiders on the brain, so there was no way I was going first! Brian led the way to clear the webs for us since he wasn't too bothered by them, and we were obviously not over our fight either, so this seemed like fair punishment to me.

Within minutes of arriving at the lookout we witnessed the most beautiful sunrise I had ever seen! Still seeing some stars in the sky, the colors started with deep blues, changing into purple, shifting dramatically into fiery red and suddenly gold as the sun peeked over the water. And the smells! The smell of the ocean was intoxicating with it's crisp salt air, vague seaweed & dead sea creature odors; plus being high up on the lush cliffs we had the dramatic smells of all the wildlife around us, full of musty, spicy and even floral smelling plants. The overall experience was more than a little overwhelming to the senses.

My photos of that sunrise are some of the most beautiful in my collection, but the photos of _us_ in front of it tell another tale…Brian looked like the seasick kid trying to make a "happy face" for the family photo on a boat after puking, and the look on _my_ face was just as transparent, only with a little more horror mixed in…since we were just at the beginning of our three month stay in this country, and those beastly spiders are _NOT_ confined to Tasmania.

6

Wine Time? Or is it Whine Time?

For a few weeks In April of 2009, my husband Brian and I were working at a winery in Australia. Now when you think of wineries Down Under, you may picture something like Napa Valley or Sonoma in California...picturesque, quaint, charming and most importantly *warm* if not *hot*. Well, this was <u>not</u> that. <u>This</u> was just outside Mt. Ararat, located in the Grampian Mountain Range. The climate more or less reminded me of the Sierra Nevada Foothills in California, complete with very temperamental fall weather in April, which is harvest season on the underbelly of the world. And by temperamental, I mean hot, dry sunburnt days, followed by freezing temperatures come nightfall accompanied by unpredictable precipitation in the form of fog, rain, sleet, hail, and whatever else nature could come up with that day.

The human powers that be, would also wait until the very last bit of warm weather hit certain hilly vineyards before harvesting them. So, sometimes there would be workers out harvesting in the 90 degree heat, while others would be sweating to death in the chemistry lab; then, with almost no notice, a storm would blow in overnight, and suddenly it was all hands on deck! Everyone would get a call at the crack of dawn to assist in harvesting another precious slope of grapes that had hit their peak in ripeness the evening before, and were suddenly threatened by surprise sleet. There might have been some order to this madness, but I didn't see it.

One particular morning was especially lousy, since it was not only storming with freezing rain, but we were called up so freakishly early, that when pre-dawn began, that bleak, half darkness stuck for hours past when it should have started bleeding into daylight. Unable to see much in those wee hours, cutting our fingers with whatever dull shears we were given was inescapable. After several hours of this slavery, Brian looked up at me, grunted something about it being our 4th wedding anniversary, then put his head back down and resumed bleeding on the crops. We didn't speak of it again for the rest of the day. I guess working at a winery together _can_ be romantic...but in my personal experiences to date, there isn't anything sexy or romantic about wine making during harvest & crush.

We hadn't quite taken into consideration all of the potential weather conditions before reaching out to this specific winery. Brian had been serving their wines in a notable Manhattan restaurant, got in touch via Email and ended up with the job. They couldn't pay him actual currency for legal reasons, but they were willing to put us up in their guest cottage on the hill, reimburse us for our gas & groceries, then send us on our merry way with wine as payment, plus some excellent stories & resume fodder. We didn't mind this bartering at all since we were going to be in the country for 3 months either way, and working for room & board was a welcome break from going into debt.

To be fair, _he_ had the job. I was neither invited, nor expected to do much actual work around the winery, since I would most likely just get in the way and make things worse for everyone. Years before, I got invited to ride shotgun down south to fetch grapes from a vineyard for a winery in Berkeley, California; and I showed up ready to pick! When I expressed my intentions to help out, the fleet of workers who arrived to actually get paid to harvest the mangled vines just gave me blank stares and then reluctantly handed me the smallest project possible to keep me out of their way. So, given this past experience, I accepted my role as keeper of the cottage and winery lookie-loo. I did however have an open invitation to join the workers daily for lunch, cooked by a timid Vietnamese woman by the name of; EyeHaveKnowIdeaHowtoEvenPronounceThat. Sometimes she would let me help her, but mostly I would just enjoy being around other humans for a while, chow down on the authentic Vietnamese food, and sit with the actual employees, getting the scoop on what those troublesome grapes & vines were up to that day.

The fella in charge of the facility was usually frustrated with something in either the weather or chemistry department, and wasn't shy about telling us all about it every opportunity he got. One day over lunch, Mr. In Charge told us that some of the newly fermenting bins had attracted vinegar flies. They would usually solve this problem with something called a "pump over" but they weren't in _those_ bins yet. So the mixing up had to be done manually...that is to say, by feet.

He devised a plan that began with me heading up the hill to our cottage for a quick, sanitizing shower, then back down to stomp on some grapes. What fun! I jumped right in, with the grapes never going further than my shins, and those flies were soon history…or at least part of the wine from that point on.

A few days later my now expert grape squashing feet services were called upon again. Following the same sanitation protocol, I arrived in my capri pants just as I had before. Mr. In Charge critically looked me up and down then asked; "have you got any *shorts?*" I'd never been big on short shorts, neither was their Vietnamese employee (whose name I still couldn't pronounce yet), so I had to borrow a pair from the only other woman working there; Kate stood several inches taller than me and was all legs, but she was busy with another time-sensitive winery task at that time…so the extra shorts she kept in her locker were available. Given my 5'4" stature, and quite the opposite body type with my short legs, I had to hike her shorts up around my ribcage like an old man before hopping into the tank. I expected to be about shin deep, instead, I began a slow-motion descent into the fermenting grape muck where I barely kept Kate's shorts in the "dry zone."

So, if any of you out there are lovers of fine Australian wine, can figure out where this place is, and get to enjoy some of their harvest from April of 2009, chances are, I've either stepped on, bled in, or smashed insects into that spectacular wine you have the privilege of enjoying. You're welcome.

7

Manhattan Wilds

In one of my previous lives, I worked as a fromager at a little cheese & wine bar called Casellula in the neighborhood of Hell's Kitchen, New York City.

For those of you who may not know what a "fromager" is, allow me to shed a little light. It's a relatively flexible term for one who might know a bit more than you do about cheese, enjoy pairing it with various condiments, and might be lucky enough to have a job styling and pairing it with various wines. That's my story, and I'm stickin' to it.

At the time, Casellula was open from 5:00 pm until 2:00 am every single day of the week. If someone walked in at 1:59 am, we would serve them. Period. That made for some late nights, but in those days, it was a party, we were all friends and nobody cared that we had to work late.

Working as the evening's fromager, one was expected to set up the cheese station with it's 35 or so cheeses, plus an endless parade of condiments; proceed to personally design and deliver each plate made throughout the evening, all while retaining enough patience to answer the same stupid questions over and over again. Fortunately, that also meant plenty of downtime since the fromager wasn't assigned a "section" of humans to maintain. Just the cheese. This also meant that the fromager would have the longest shift of any front of the house person since they had to take full responsibility for leaving the station exactly the way they found it. Thankfully, we never served lunch. I mean, we served a "weekend brunch" for a spell in 2008, but that was a disaster and after that *#&%$hitshow got canceled, we never spoke of it again.

One Saturday night in early fall of 2011, around one o'clock in the morning, I was washing my hands behind the bar, chatting with my boss and his friend Kate; when all of the sudden out of nowhere I saw a goat across the street outside causally trotting up 52nd St. towards a busy 9th Avenue! *Naturally,* I abandoned my post to chase after this creature who was certainly headed towards a gruesome catastrophe.

I darted out from behind the bar, around the cheese station, past the bathroom, dodging guests, tables, chairs and my confused co-workers on my way out the door! By the time I finally caught up with the goat in question, she had miraculously crossed the busy intersection all by herself. She had a leash on, but nobody seemed to be in charge of holding the other end. After stepping on the leash to gain control of the animal, I quickly scanned through the throngs of people on the street at that late hour, and nobody seemed to really take note of us. I couldn't help but think to myself; *"Come on New York, really? How is nobody seeing this right now?"*

Instead of pointlessly searching for her handler, I simply decided to take this creature back to the restaurant for a while. I mean, we had a tree out front with a little dirt around it, and I *did* have a fenced in, private backyard across the river in Hoboken where I could keep her over the weekend at least. I began to wonder to myself; *"Is it even legal for me to keep a goat in my backyard? How long before I would be turned in? What would my punishment be? How would I get her home? Can you take a goat on the subway? What about Uber? I have a hard enough time getting a driver to take my dog, I'm sure they'd have something to say about a goat."*

Snapping back to the present reality, I realized that walking wasn't an option, all my friends in New York were intentionally car-free, and my New Jersey friends were probably all asleep at this hour like responsible adults. I considered the ferry for a moment, but then remembered that they stopped at 11:00 pm on the weekends and I wouldn't be getting out of work until 2:15 am at the earliest. At least I would have an hour or two to ponder the predicament and maybe even get some others to brainstorm with me to come up with an acceptable plan.

By the time I got back to the restaurant, my boss and Kate were casually leaning against the railing leading up to the front door and doing quite an unconvincing job of stifling their laughter. Looking down, I suddenly realized how absurd I looked. Dressed in a black & white empire waisted dress with spaghetti straps, black smock-style apron, a faded green, ancient bandana covering my hair pulled back into a bun fit for a peasant, black clogs on my feet, and now I've got a goat on a leash.

Ignoring their comments and now unbridled laughter, I tied her to the tree outside and resumed my job inside, which was, after all, serving cheese to hungry people at this tiny, overcrowded restaurant in the middle of Manhattan.

The restaurant had hit a lul before I dashed out the door, so my orders hadn't piled up all too badly, and nobody complained when I explained to them that the reason for their less than speedy service was due to a goat, and the proof was right outside.

While I was playing catch-up, I decided that this goat needed a name, not having too much time to think about it, I decided on Sophie.

We started to get a late night throng of guests consisting of mostly our theater friends...this was, after all, Casellula. Everyone here has been crowding some sort of center stage since _birth_, and this was the fabulous wave of hungry folks coming to us for nourishment after they had finished signing autographs and taking pictures with their adoring fans. I knew just about all of them by sight, but hadn't had the privilege of seeing most of their shows. (One of the cruel realities of restaurant work, the hours generally overlap the theater.) I suppose they were all famous to some degree, but all I really cared about in this situation was knowing exactly what sort of cheese & wine they liked, remembering what they had last time, all of their allergies, and whether or not they will want water glasses taking up their precious table space.

Naturally a goat tied up outside their favorite establishment raised _all_ the questions, and I was more than happy to get their creative juices flowing by asking them if they had any bright ideas for getting her to my home in New Jersey. Ideas are like wildfire, and pretty soon the whole restaurant was aflame with conversation and scheming over my little Sophie.

One generous friend suggested we take her to his apartment and wait for daylight when folks might be a little more open to goat transportation.

Another creative schemer insisted that he "knows a guy" who will do it, but only under the cover of complete darkness, shrouded in secrecy.

Yet another declared that we should simply take her to the lock-in bar we've been known to patronize after hours...I mean, if they're locking the door and serving people illegally they might not mind that we had a goat in tow.

None of these really sounded like a stellar idea, since they would all involve an all-nighter with an irresponsible amount of booze, and I had to work a 10 hour shift the following day. Not to mention, I had a husband, a 13 oz chinchilla and a 100 lb dog who *might* not be thrilled at such behavior...not without being invited at least. *Pretty sure* my husband wouldn't mind an all nighter with a good story, the chinchilla would most likely ignore the goat completely, and my dog would probably enjoy a backyard buddy. However, it's not all that smart to make these types of late night decisions based on "pretty sure" "most likely" and "probably".

Unfortunately all of our hair-brained ideas came crashing down when the fella to whom Sophie belonged, came looking for her. Finding her tied up, you'd think he'd be furious, but he laughed it off and in the end he thanked me for keeping her safe for a few hours. He had ducked into a bar to use the toilet, got stuck talking to a neighborhood friend, someone bought him a drink, and when he came back she had gotten loose. Who really knows how much of that is true, or how long she was left alone for, I didn't feel like challenging this guy's story, especially given the late hour. I just hope Sophie and her fella are still living together happily in some tiny apartment somewhere in Manhattan.

And that's how the story might have gone *IF* the goat's owner hadn't been walking 10 feet ahead of her when I caught up and grabbed her leash. At which point the man turned around and clearly stated "it's okay, she's with me!"

What REALLY happened:

I caught up with the goat after she did indeed cross the busy intersection, I stepped on the leash she was wearing, and from about 10 feet ahead of us a guy hollered out to us, "it's okay, she's with me!" Incredibly disappointed, I trudged back to the bar where Brian and Kate were standing outside waiting for me to return. In his snarkiest tone, Brian asked me, "So, Jamie. Did you catch the goat?" By this time, Katie was giggling uncontrollably, while I responded with; "Why yes Brian, I caught the goat. But she was with someone." He proceeded to question me further, "So, what was your plan?" Only slightly embarrassed, but mostly disappointed, I stormed back to my work station and didn't stop speculating about it for the rest of the night...all alone, in my head.

8

Stay in Your Lane

From 2014 - 2018, my husband Brian and I owned a little cheese & wine tavern in Jersey City called Third & Vine. We had originally hired our dear friend Lynn Wheeler to be our _consulting_ chef; but by the time we opened, we had come up with an agreeable financial arrangement with perks mixed in, so that he was able to live on what we could afford to pay him...therefore, he stayed on with us full time and became our biggest asset.

We had each worked with Lynn in various restaurants in New York City, lived in the same neighborhood of Manhattan for a span of years, spent several holidays together and were basically family by the time we opened on Valentine's Day, 2014. Brian even got ordained for the primary purpose of marrying Lynn and his partner Ric at the restaurant a few years into our venture. Brian had fun with that one too! Since back then, when you got ordained through the Universal Life Church Online, they encouraged you to choose your title from their master list; he had a tough time choosing between "Universal Philosopher of Absolute Reality", and "Rock God." He decided that "Rock

God" was too vague, so he went for the former.

Additionally, we would close to the public every Halloween so we could host Lynn & Ric's annual drag show; "HallowQueen Dragstravaganza". This event was a special perk for everyone involved, since they would hire their own bouncer, Lynn would prepare all the food, Ric would sell all the tickets and the bouncer was left to deal with cover charges and keeping out any unwanted riff-raff. All Brian and I had to do was schedule a bartender, dress up, sit back and enjoy the show. And believe me, on Halloween night in a relatively big city, that was a welcome break for the management team of "just the three of us"; plus a solid bonus for the lucky bartender who pulled that shift.

Now Lynn was neither tall, nor short, a little on the round side and a lot on the quiet side. He maintained his serenity more than any chef I've ever worked with, never backed down on his musical choices in the kitchen (which was _always_ Pride Radio by the way), supported every single person working alongside him, and ran one of the cleanest kitchens in Jersey City at the time. When faced with a slightly uncomfortable situation, he would display his best maitre'd facade and proceed as though everything was under control, until it was, indeed, under control. His eyes might get a little wide behind his glasses from time to time, but that's as close to panic as I'd ever see him.

At Third & Vine, my husband Brian ran the complex bar, with constantly evolving cocktails, the most confusing and interesting wine list he could wrangle together, plus a rotating focus on different types of booze to both educate and impress our adoring public. I ran the extensive cheese program, with a list of 25 cheeses on the menu, and several "gray market" cheeses on an invisible secret menu, each paired up with an array of condiments I would mostly make myself. And Lynn managed the kitchen situation with a stabilized menu, plus seasonal items added in for a dash of fun with a side of "how in the world did you think of that?" Or "why in the world would you put those two things together?" Always with a conclusion of "Wow! What kind of sorcery made that so darn delicious?!"

Being zookeepers of each of our departments, the way we all managed to not kill each other over those 4 years was to stay out of each other's domains and allow one another to run our respective spaces with minimal micro-managing. We didn't always do a good job at staying out of each other's business, but hey, what kind family doesn't have it's problems? We were all extremely passionate about our specialties, dedicated to the highest quality possible and maybe a little obsessed with perfection. If we had the capacity to come up with a team motto, it may have looked a little something like:

"Stay in your lane, do your best, trust each other, and make every guest feel like family."

We tried hiring people with the same standards, which naturally was hit & miss, but mostly a big hit! With *very* few exceptions, our employees were all worth their weight in gold.

One bustling Friday night at Third & Vine, I was playing the role of hostess. In those days, it was far easier to train someone how to make cheese plates than it was to find someone with the skills required to run our waiting list without either going mad, or upsetting a guest. Therefore, I most often had to change hats to manage this post. Fulfilling this role on the weekends could be an exasperating chore since, while we were *technically* a restaurant serving dinner, we were also very much a *bar* where folks tended to sit, graze, and enjoy one another's company; all while watching the movies we played on silent with subtitles... often lingering for *hours*, making it nearly impossible for me to inform the folks waiting with any certainty "how long" the wait was going to be for a seat.

On the night in question, I was running a 45 minute wait for *any* spot, be it at the bar, a communal table, whatever. 45 minutes to sit your rear end in *any* chair.

The previous owner of the space had foolishly placed the one and only bathroom near the front door, where anyone off the street could easily sneak in and use the facilities without buying anything. We tried to avoid such behavior, but when someone would ask *nicely* we were of course accommodating. After all, it was better than having them relieve themselves on the streets, which was not unheard of in a city like ours...anyone who has ever walked downtown in an urban area knows exactly what I am talking about. Cities don't naturally smell like urine, humans mostly do that.

About two hours after sundown, out of nowhere, pushing through the crowd gathered near the front door, emerged a slightly homeless smelling, twitchy dude with long, dreadlocked hair and sunglasses on. He was clearly not a rockstar, so the sunglasses indoors, after dark, were a dead giveaway that something unusual was about to happen. Not exactly sure if he was drunk, high, off his meds, or some combination of these factors, I proceeded with hospitality laced with caution; "Good evening sir, how can I help you?" He gestured with his hand cupped around an invisible glass, raising it to his lips a few times in succession , "drink...I need a drink." Politely, I offered to get him some water. He, repeating the same gesture as before, replied, "Nah, nah, nah man...drink. I need a drink." I repeated that I'd be happy to get him some water, but it would be at least an hour before we could serve him any alcohol at the bar. At the time I was serving alcoholic beverages to the rest of the folks standing around while they were waiting, but sometimes when you run a bar you just have to glaze over the truth and hope nobody notices.

As I was offering this man water for the last time, Chef Lynn emerged from the bathroom behind me and touched my shoulder, letting me know he was there to support me during whatever might go down. I knew just enough about dealing with unpredictable humans to know that it's usually _not_ the best idea to bring in a man, to try and talk down another man. But it was nice to know Lynn was there to defend me verbally, or throw a punch if things went that direction.

After what felt like an eternity, the man gave up and headed for the door. When he successfully arrived outside, the whole front room erupted in applause! A few of our guests told me that they had seen this guy around town before, and one couple commented that they'd never seen _anyone_ get him to leave on his own before. Well then! Bravo to me! But my triumph was cut short when a few seconds later, he was back; this time without his sunglasses on. I froze, thinking, _"he's just had a few minutes to think about it, maybe realized he kinda got rejected, and is coming back to settle the score"._ But he just looked at me as though he'd never seen me before and began miming a rectangle shape around his eyes with his thumbs and index fingers muttering "man, my shades…my shades man, I left my shades in the bathroom." I responded with, "Sir, you never made it to the bathroom. Please check your pockets." He paused, patted himself down, discovered the pocket where his shades must have crawled into on their own, lit up with more enthusiasm than I thought he was capable of, placed his shades back on his face and proudly marched back out the door.

Once again the whole front room erupted in applause, this time peppered with surprised laughter! I'm sure the guy, now standing right outside, thought he must have done something amazing to deserve such a reaction from the crowd. This time I ran to the door and bolted it…right there in the middle of service on a busy night. I've never been big on confrontation to begin with, and I'd had quite enough for one day.

9

Thank You Captain Hindsight

In August of 2018 I was on a train from New York City to Pittsburgh, PA to attend the American Cheese Society Conference for the first time. The first year I had even *heard* of the conference was in 2007 when I had my first full time, cheese-focused job as a *fromager at a little cheese & wine cafe in Manhattan called Casellula.

Each year there was a different reason for me to stay behind; "The Senior Fromager needs to go." Or "Chef needs to go." Or "the Pastry Chef needs to go." My only consolation was knowing that in the end, they really needed to leave behind "Jamie the workhorse" to help run things while all the more important people were away for their long weekend of cheesy fun & fancy parties

By the time I finally opened my own wine & cheese tavern with my husband Brian in 2014, we simply didn't have the staff to take *any* weekends off. *If* and *when* we took a weekend off, it had to be for seriously important family functions, like a wedding or a funeral...certainly *NOT* for going to taste and learn more about cheeses. After working as owner/operators of our establishment for 4 years and getting sober in 2017, we finally decided to find an acceptable buyer and take our leave of the business. Owning and running a bar in sobriety, _sucks_...at least it did for us. But anywho, after being unable to attend the cheese conference for 11 years, I was understandably quite eager to finally see what all the fuss was about.

We were still living in the apartment above our sold establishment in Jersey City, NJ, and the conference was just 368 miles to the west in Pittsburgh, PA. Brian had grown up in Northern NJ and went to college in Pittsburgh, so he was familiar with how mind & butt-numbing the drive could be, therefore we decided to take the train. We've always preferred to travel by train whenever possible...we realized this when we moved cross-country from San Francisco to New York in 2005 by way of Amtrak. Growing up in the Sierra Nevada mountains, trains were a delightful novelty to me, while with Brian's Northeastern upbringing, taking the train was as mundane as calling for a taxi. We didn't agree on much back then, but taking the train anywhere was something we could easily agree on...he could be as bored as he wanted, work on his latest knitting project, catch up on the news and fall asleep...whilst I could read, write, gaze out at the countryside, and text with my friends & family.

On the train, a few hours away from our destination, I bit into a sandwich, and a tooth that I had been babying for over 2 years finally came all the way out! When I originally knocked it loose in a drunken episode sometime in 2015, the infernal thing stayed attached to my lower cluster of front teeth by way of the "permanent retainer" my orthodontist had put there when I was 14. So when the tooth came loose, it wasn't _really out_...just dead, unstable and sitting there held in with some glue, wire and rotting roots.

I was fairly new to being a sober adult human at the time, and the thought of facing this particular problem from my past was too much for me. I figured I'd just take care of it when it got bad enough...I just hadn't planned "bad enough" coming to pass on my way to an important conference where I would not only see my old boss, but possibly every notable person in the cheese business in the Americas. The upside to this, was I only knew 1 person there, and once he quit making fun of me, nobody else seemed to notice. The missing tooth was from my lower choppers, I already have a slight overbite and I realized after a while that as long as it's not a "front and center" tooth, a small gap in your smile isn't all that noticeable, especially if you can remember to make eye contact.

My lactard husband understandably had zero interest in the cheese conference, so he kept to himself and explored Pittsburg while I proceeded to enjoy myself to the fullest, attached at the hip to my new found friend Jen! At that time, Jen was the Chef at Casellula, the place where I had worked very happily for years *right* before Jen took over the kitchen. Like two ships passing in the night, we both had worked at Casellula for years, just during different times and simply missed each other. We met up at the recommendation of one of my favorite people in the whole world, Leigh. Now Leigh was the Pastry Chef at Casellula at the time, and had been a part of my life both professionally and personally since 2007, so I trusted her judgment when she suggested that Jen and I buddy up at the conference.

Jen, and I were like two peas in a pod, and she never gave me grief over my irregular grin. As fate would have it, that friendship deepened and grew, and within 4 months, when Casellula was in a jam, I was offered my old job back...only better since I would only have to do the jobs I liked, and almost nothing I didn't. And just like that, the dream team was formed!

I had been sober for about a year and a half by that time, and was still wallowing in my guilt, fear & shame…like, a lot. So I decided to ignore the gap in my smile for another 6 months, knowing I was in for at least one implant to fix my appearance.

I had heard from more than a dozen people that having major dental work done in Mexico or Costa Rica was a much more affordable option for us Americans with our lousy excuse for any kind of insurance.

I found out that I would need to begin this process by Emailing X-rays to whomever I chose. So I began my search for a local dentist who would simply X-ray my mandible, give me the digital copies and send me on my merry way.

After calling around to several recommended offices and hearing their quotes, I decided to check out New York University's Dental School. I was under the impression that for those without dental insurance, becoming a patient at a dental school can be an affordable option. Plus, I figured they would be open to the simple "get my X-rays and run" idea I had come up with.

This turned out to be one of the most expensive, and longest medical processes I've ever dealt with, *and I broke my back in three places when I was 18.*

First of all, it took me over an hour just to get there…biking to downtown Jersey City, locking up my bike and taking the train. Then, taking the bus as far as I could, then making the rest of my pilgrimage on foot. Thankfully, I started this whole process in the spring, so braving winter conditions wouldn't prove to be an additional problem.

My first appointment was merely a consultation to establish my eligibility. After that I had to come back for X-rays.

Getting those X-rays was incredibly frustrating and uncomfortable, since I was, after all, dealing with students. And these particular students didn't seem to have an active supervisor who cared at all about my comfort, feelings or peace of mind. Students also don't have to worry themselves over things like being kind or at the very least feigning politeness in order to keep you coming back as a patient. They tell it like it is (or at least how they perceive it), in all their young, arrogant NYU+NYC smugness...and with the exception of 1 person (who had an "Uncle Drunkie" in the family) I didn't get any pats on the back, points, or shiny gold stars for my recovery, or being sober *NOW*, facing my problems and trying to do better. There was only active shaming.

After the X-ray party that lasted for over 2 hours, I was informed that they would be holding my X-rays hostage until I had committed to a deep clean. After some thought, I figured it might be a good idea to just go with it since at that point in my life, I hadn't actually seen a dentist for at least two decades. So I agreed, and they _finally_ released the X-rays into my possession!

I left this gaggle of judgmental snobs with my prognosis; I would indeed return for a full deep cleaning, which meant coming back for a total of 4 visits where I would only get ¼ of my mouth tortured at a time. But at least I finally had my X-rays and could begin the process of finding _real_ experts. _Anywhere_ but there.

2 weeks later I was back for my first official round of suffering. "For teaching purposes" I would have the same "dentist" every time. That is, the same, humorless, flailing student desperately trying to scrape my teeth & gums down to the bone in order to satisfy a teacher for a good grade.

Laying there in anguish, all I could do was thank God for my high pain tolerance while trying not to tear up. I learned at a relatively young age that I'm one of those weirdos who *"over-feels" everything* but apparently has an unusually high tolerance for it. (I learned _much_ later in life that this is true for me on more than one level.)

You'd think after this intimate experience with my "dentist" I'd remember his name, but I've obviously blocked it out, so let's just call him "Joe". He was a nice enough kid, going into dentistry to serve in the Army. Perfect, so I've got the guy actually going to school to learn how to torture soldiers. Now, I've never had to survive boot camp, but after 4 appointments with "Joe" I consider myself an honorary cadet.

After completing my excruciating deep clean over a 4 month period, I was finally able to sit with an actual teaching dentist to go over my options. He had students in tow, so he was just radiating the boldest dental shaming persona I'd witnessed to date. After hearing him out while trying not to cry or scream, I politely gave him the brush-off line of "let me think about it, and I'll call the office when I've decided". As it turned out, for the price of what needed to be done, I could have a breezy vacation in Costa Rica and do it all for less than half the quoted NYU price.

I'd heard about this place in Costa Rica called Nova Dental when I was working one night at Casellula as their fromager. Casellula was open well past midnight every night, so we attracted an extremely high number of restaurant workers coming in late and hungry after their shifts. One of my regulars, Dana, was one of these gems. She arrived late one Sunday night. Alone. This was only odd because she usually had Justin, her fiancé in tow.

I came to find out that Justin had scheduled _his_ dental implants to be done in Costa Rica a few weeks before, and they were going to make the trip together so that she could take care of him during his recovery period post-surgery. *Only* when they arrived at the airport did they realize she had gotten tickets for San Jose, California instead of San Jose, Costa Rica! They decided to make the most of the situation, rescheduled the dental work and enjoyed a surprise visit to California. Unfortunately she had used up all *her* vacation days accidentally going to California, and since Justin worked for himself, *his* boss was totally cool with him taking another week off to try again.

This time Justin brought his mother along to help nurse his recovery. So there she was, sitting there alone at the bar, her fiancé in Costa Rica with his mother, Dana enjoying her cheese & wine in New York and unable to keep a straight face while she explained this blunder to me!

She of course promised to let me know how Justin liked "Nova Dental" since I was in the market, and would kill for a personal recommendation! Upon returning from Costa Rica a few weeks later, Justin had nothing but nice things to say about Nova Dental. So in October of 2019 I packed my bags and hit the skies.

I was a little wary of having such a major ordeal done all alone, so I asked my mother to join me. This way I would have someone to be with me post-surgery in case I needed assistance. Mom was coming from California, I was coming from New Jersey, and our planes were destined to arrive in San Jose, Costa Rica within an hour of each other.

Now I've had my fair share of long travel days, but this one takes the cake! Without realizing it, I had accidentally scheduled a 13 hour layover in Mexico City. Not a huge deal since I'm pretty good at amusing myself in airports, but I was confined to a small section of the airport, and my limited Spanish wasn't of much use. Thankfully almost everyone in the airport spoke English, so the first 12 hours weren't the worst.

After locating my gate an hour before my flight, they announced a major delay due to weather in Costa Rica...I couldn't understand much of anything coming over the P.A., So I picked 2 distinctive people who were on my flight and followed them around as the gates kept changing. I must have seemed like such a creeper, but I was lost and alone, so I didn't care how it looked. By this time the airport shops had all closed down, and I was down to my last power bar. Pretty sure the vending machines worked, but I had all the wrong currency, and didn't want to actually consume anything they were offering. I also didn't exactly trust water from the fountains, so thus began my accidental fasting & dehydration process.

We ended up being delayed another 5 hours. I tried getting in touch with my mom, to give her an update, but her phone kept going straight to voicemail and she wasn't returning any of my texts. As for my "distinctive people"; one was a tall, willowy dude flaunting a man-bun hauling around a guitar. The other was a short, scrawny young lady sporting a yellow sundress and clinging to her chihuahua...each of them obviously flashing their prized possessions for all to see. I followed them around for another 3 gate changes, and by the time we all finally got on our rickety old plane and jostled our way through the still terrifying storm to San Jose, I was over the moon to finally be at my destination... well, maybe, "over the moon" is the wrong phrase; more like exhausted, punchy, starved and relieved.

Naturally when I arrived, I made another attempt to get in touch with my mother, who should have arrived hours before me by this time. When she finally picked up the phone she was all "Hey! Guess where I am?!" "The Hotel?" I guessed....to which she replied, "Nope! Panama!" Her flight was affected by the local storm, same as mine (duh) but since her flight was coming from further away and was already in the air, instead of being delayed like mine, it simply got diverted...to Panama. The airline put her entire plane of passengers up in a hotel "overnight", (which in reality was only like 5 hours of not being in the airport) and took excellent care of them, even though NOBODY was able to access their luggage...unfortunately they were stuck with whatever they had in their carry-ons. This was when mom started carrying a toothbrush with her at all times.

So while mom enjoyed a spontaneous, short visit to Panama, I was left to fend for myself in Costa Rica. In the middle of the night. During a tropical storm.

Thankfully Nova Dental had referred me to Las Cumbres Inn for my stay, and _they_ had recommended a driver by the name of Carlos who would become my chauffeur and friend for the remainder of my stay. He picked me up from the airport without incident, and was extremely gracious considering my 6 hour delay that had landed me there well past midnight. We arrived at the inn, and after I gave him my schedule of appointments, he left...insisting that I needn't bother to pay him until the end of the week, and that I needed to get some rest before tomorrow's big day.

The owner of the inn was a voluptuous, vibrant, rotund & tall Costa Rican with very large hair, a beaming smile and giant eyes. If it wasn't for her kind face and calm demeanor she might have been ominous & intimidating. But, she was extremely hospitable and friendly to me during my check-in, despite the fact that she had been woken up by a phone call in the middle of the night from Carlos to let us in.

She walked me outside and down the steps in the pouring rain and thick darkness to the suite I had booked apart from the main entrance; then the key she gave me broke off in the lock. By this time I was just so DONE with the last 24 hours, all I could do was laugh at it. We both did. Then she redirected me to a tiny room back inside the inn for the night, and assured me they would fix the lock in the morning and I'd have my suite by the time I got back from my first appointment.

The next morning Carlos picked me up and we made it to Nova Dental with time to spare! I had thought that the first day would be a consultation, giving me a day or so to mentally prepare myself (aka psych myself out). But I was wrong; they would be doing the surgery just as soon as I filled my prescription for the pain around the corner. I had also assumed they would be knocking me out for my procedure, but oh how wrong I was yet again! I got through my surgery, fully awake but surprisingly with almost zero pain due to an innovative system for anesthesia called "The Wand". It uses state of the art, contact free numbing; nothing like those barbaric needles they use in the States. Here and there I felt a little pain and I squirmed. Then they would "wand" me again, and I felt nothing but a subtle vibration in my jaw. I could then go back to watching with curiosity the strange soap opera they put on the tv that was affixed to the ceiling. After it was over, Carlos picked me up yet again to take me back to the inn where mom was, at long last, there waiting for me.

After swapping stories, mom and I proceeded to just goof off for the next 5 days of "recovery". We played cards, ate some amazing food, and watched movies. We even dipped our toes in the pool, but it never warmed up quite enough for either of us to want to get in. The meds they gave me for the pain didn't cause any nausea or tiredness like I had expected, so while I didn't _need_ my mommy, it was nice to have her company.

In the end, a few ladies learned some important things from our South American flight experiences; For Dana, she learned to check the country of her destination. For mom, she learned to _always_ keep a few "essentials" such as a toothbrush and possibly a change of underwear in your carry-on. And for me, I learned to always, and I mean _always_ carry your own snacks.

*"Fromager": Fancy name for "cheese stylist" or "cheesemonger" this job in particular, was at a wine bar. For a slightly expanded explanation, chapter 7; paragraph 2.

10

Westward: Never a "Jersey Girl"

In January of 2020 my younger brother Andrew and his wife Amy moved me across the country from Jersey City, New Jersey to Copperopolis, California. So basically from a bustling Manhattan suburb, to the middle of absolutely nowhere. I had planned on making this move much later in May of 2020 with my mom; leisurely visiting friends, hitting up the Over The Rhine music festival in Ohio, leaving space for plenty of detours, and really making a road trip out of it! But, due to a series of blunders and major hiccups in my personal life, everything suddenly changed and I just had to get on with my next chapter.

My immediate family all lived on the west coast at the time, so moving there made perfect sense to me, and my aging grandmother, recently widowed, needed a buddy, and most likely in the future, a chauffeur & personal assistant, so I would be moving in with her.

My whole family _really_ pitched in to make it happen with plane tickets, cash and a boatload of prayers, but Andrew and Amy were the ones with enough free time and energy to fly out and help with the actual moving part. My older brother,

Nick was all married with 3 kids, plus a demanding job at the time. My younger sister, Annika was also married, had recently relocated back to California from overseas, plus was pregnant with her 4th child. My mother was on a long awaited "bucket list" trip in Israel, and my father doesn't get on a plane unless someone has died.

Now, Andrew is my twin. Not literally, we're more like twins born 5 years apart. We get each other in ways that blow my mind to this very day. Our personalities are different enough, but for some reason we have this uncanny connection as siblings. Perhaps it has something to do with the fact that we've both battled with addiction, been through the ringer with lousy romantic relationships, and faced what feels like more than our fair share of pain & loss. All of which brought us to incredibly low places at one time or another, from which point we had to fight & claw our way back up to health, healing and overall sanity. Not without help of course, but those stories are written elsewhere. The point is, we have a special bond.

When Andrew met and married his wife Amy in 2019, I was delighted to discover that she fit into our family like a long lost glove. Being both spiritually grounded and entertaining, together they embody joy and a boundless love for life. They practically manufacture happiness and devour positive experiences. They also crave spontaneity, so having them around during decision making time is a guarantee to never face a dull moment.

When they came to fetch me, we had no idea how we were going to get me back home, so the road trip was a crazy, spontaneous whirlwind decision and we decided to just "wing it". We knew at least one thing ahead of time; and that was that we didn't want to challenge my front wheel drive city car or the U-Haul we would have to rent with extreme weather or terrain…so the southern route was the most obvious. We had each crossed this great expanse of a country several times, both alone and with others, but never with a U-Haul. And NEVER with a 100 lb Bernese Mountain Dog. Her name was Pepper.

Years ago, at the suggestion of a brilliant ferry boat captain in New York, I decided to have Pepper registered as a "service animal". Please understand, I did NOT do it to be an asshole; and if she wasn't a well behaved creature I would never have even considered it. But being the obedient love bug she was, I did it. Don't judge me. Besides, it came in handy countless times in her 11 years with me! Especially when we were homeless for a month after hurricane Sandy struck the east coast in 2012, and Hoboken pooped inside my house. But that's a story for another time.

I knew we could use her status as a "service dog" to get away with staying in any motel we chose. But, ever the peacemaker, I decided to make an effort to avoid any possibility of excess drama, so I chose a dog friendly motel chain. For the sake of the story, let's just call it the Red WOOF.

While we were packing up my apartment, Andrew and Amy taught me about "Sneaky Cards." They had started this with my nieces in Reno, and it's just good, clean, goofy FUN! Simply put, it's a pack of playing cards that demand actions…mostly aimed at strangers. They say things like: "Give this card to someone in uniform", or "hide this card inside someone's desk", or "start a dance party using the hokey pokey, the first one to join you, gets this card". You get the picture. The point is, you can register the deck, hand out the cards, hope the recipient of the card follows the instructions and keeps the game going. I've heard of these cards traveling more than most Americans do in their entire lives. So, with great reserve in my heart, I agreed to play the game across the country. Thankfully it was January of 2020, RIGHT before such behavior would have been treated with unprecedented hostility. (See *Covid-19...who am I kidding? There is no footnote. We still have google right?)

Thursday, January 23rd:

After spending only 4 days packing up everything I intended to move with, the three of us went to pick up the U-Haul, and as soon as we drove in we saw this truck with a GIANT green garden spider painted on it's side. Andrew jokingly declared "There she is! That one is OURS!" I shuddered, then laughed it off because I hate spiders more than anything, and there is no way I want to drive across the entire country with one on my stuff!

As we pulled around we spotted another truck getting prepped up for a drive...it was a charming, clean little thing with a horse drawn carriage painted on it's side. "There, that's more like it!" I said. "That just has to be the one for us." I'd been holding my breath without realizing it, and at the moment I laid eyes on that beautiful second truck, I was so relieved that I immediately relaxed and started breathing again.

By my choice, Andrew and Amy would be the only ones authorized to drive the giant vehicle. In my 38 years on this earth I had spent 20 of them living in cities where I had no need of a car, let my license expire for 7 of those years, and had only recently started driving again. So I was a little shy to drive a U-Haul, besides, I had my tiny little 4 door hatchback to drive, and I like my alone time.

After filling out all the paperwork and getting a lecture about all the potential dangers of driving a U-Haul (thus confirming my decision *NOT* to be a driver) they handed Andrew the keys and we headed out to fetch our truck...as it turned out, Andrew was right, we got the first one we saw; so yeah, I now get to move all the way across the country, following a giant spider.

Next came the business of naming her. I enjoy naming things; always have. It used to be restricted to critters and plants, but that changed a few years ago when my older brother Nick introduced me to a very special podcast..."Everything is Alive" is an unscripted interview show in which all the subjects are inanimate objects. In each episode, a different object, complete with a personal name, tells us its life story; and everything it says has to be true. I already wanted to name everything, and this just compounded my desires. When I got my red, 2014 Nissan hatchback in 2019 I decided to call her Ruby Von Rhodes. (When she's misbehaving I call her The Red Menace.) The "Von" part was especially funny since I also had a 17 year old chinchilla, named Duchess Gertrude Von Puffybottom the Third, and thanks to some German dog breeder, my 100lb dog's name on her legal papers reads Nessie Vom Schafshugel.

We decided to keep it simple for the U-Haul and name her Charlotte, after one of my favorite childhood cartoons, Charlotte's Web. (How a cartoon about a message delivering, procreating, giant spider, got to be a favorite of mine as a kid, is beyond my current comprehension.)

We returned to the apartment to pack up Charlotte and have one last good, solid night of sleep before getting on our way early the next morning. The flighty roommates I had foolishly allowed to move in with me in October, were able to take over my non-existent lease, and even offered to "buy" some of the things I had chosen to leave behind, so thankfully the apartment wasn't completely barren.

Without a doubt, Andrew, Amy & I ended up staying up _way too late_ that night playing games and dreaming out loud all about the fun we were about to have on this epic road trip...because, after all, we are Maynes, and that sometimes means that we run on very little sleep, all in the name of "bonding".

Friday, January 24th:

Our first stop was just around the corner at Gia Gelato & Cafe; the best place for breakfast in Jersey City at the time. Debbie, the owner of the Cafe, was working the counter, and served up the most beautiful cups of coffee & breakfast sammiches I'd ever seen.

With happy/sad tears in my eyes, I bid farewell to Debbie and Jersey City for the last time. Ripping out roots and saying goodbye is always hard. And this was especially rough for me at the time since I had lived in the area for 15 years, made countless friends, owned a popular bar/restaurant in the heart of downtown for 4 of those years, sold it to someone who ran it into the ground while I had a front row seat, survived a painful divorce, and began my journey into yoga and healing through movement.

So there we were, 3 sleep deprived, but fully caffeinated Maynes, 1 big black dog, 1 tiny red car and 1 giant green spider on a U-Haul...all setting out for the adventure of a lifetime!

11

Westward: Pronouncing "Arkansas"

That first night landed us in Bristol, Virginia where we checked into our first Red WOOF. Checking in was _almost_ drama free, with only a slight annoyance that they charged $7.00 for the third person in the room...no charge for the animal, and even though a third person would be much less likely chew anything up, probably not poop on the floor or put any other extra strains on the economics of the stay, the charge was still "a thing" in my mind where I felt a strong sense of injustice.

The room was lovely. The doors were even on the inside of the building instead of outside, as I would usually expect from this tier of motel. There were even tiny little signs posted around the room, politely stating; "If you forgot anything, please don't hesitate to call the front desk and it will be provided for you with our compliments if possible."

I was quite impressed with the charming atmosphere, high quality and hospitality of this place. So we all agreed we'd continue to stay at this particular chain the whole trip if possible, _plus_ sign up for their rewards program, which boasted of a "Stay two nights get the third night FREE!!" Since we were going to be on the road for a little under a week, this seemed like a good idea at the time. So after planning our next day, we rearranged the furniture ever so slightly to enable us to play a bit of cards...as is the way of the Mayne Tribe.

Saturday, January 25th:

I woke up the next morning at the crack of 6:30 with an anxious Pepper who desperately wanted to go out! Scrambling for my shoes, I opened the motel room door dressed in what might pass for pajamas in a trailer park setting, and Pepper came nose to nose with the tallest Whippet-type-looking dog I'd ever seen! Knowing these dogs can easily get overexcited, I was grateful when this creature turned out to be quite docile. I groggily mumbled something I can't remember in greeting to the handler and we went on our way; Pepper was on a mission. We found the back entrance, designed that way so you don't have to go by the front desk for pet relief, and I suddenly got a brilliant idea! At the next motel, we could check in as two, then sneak the third party in the back door to avoid that $7 fee! I get some of my best ideas when Pepper is pooping.

While we were all getting ready for our day, it somehow came up that none of us had ever been to a Cracker Barrel Restaurant! Feeling the need to experience this supposed novelty, we hit up a location in Kingsport, Tennessee for breakfast. At the time we were under the impression that Cracker Barrel was unique to the eastern half of the country. We noticed later that we were dead wrong about this assumption. They are *EVERYWHERE*.

The young lady at the host stand took Pepper's service animal card to her manager for inspection, and within minutes, we were happily seated. The staff and customers alike were thrilled to have her! Never in my adult-dog-owning life had I ever felt so welcomed with my fur-ball. And she was perfectly well behaved...although that might have had something to do with the bacon I had slipped into my pocket from Debbie's the day before...just in case.

Over breakfast we also realized that we were headed straight for Nashville, TN. Amy couldn't bear the thought of *avoiding* the city for any reason...I mean, we're just so close! How could we NOT "stop by"?! She convinced me by finding a place to have lunch called the Grilled Cheeserie. By this point, my professional life for the last 20 years had been geared towards cheese. Cheese service, cheese making, cheese styling, private cheese catering, even owning a cheese & wine tavern...and Amy clearly took advantage of this in her persuasive argument to "stop by" Nashville.

The Grilled Cheeserie turned out to be one restaurant in a sort of indoor/outdoor food court. Brilliant! And yes, I'd absolutely make it a staple if I lived there; and once again, Pepper was a superstar, and this time extremely popular with the kids. Funny how people perceive her in cowboy country though, at a dainty 100 lbs, she's more often mistaken for a fat Collie than a small Berner.

The place where we sat in this indoor/outdoor marvel, was next to an ice cream place. To say my family is obsessed with ice cream would be a gross understatement...and it comes from BOTH sides of the family. My paternal grandparents were obsessed with an ice cream parlor near where they lived in California called Feltons Creamery; *plus* they always had an over abundance of ice cream in their 3 freezers. And my maternal grandparents were famous for the home-made, hand-cranked ice cream they would make almost daily whenever visitors came during the summer months. They *also* kept an unnatural amount of ice cream stashed away in _their_ 5 freezers.

So naturally, when we got halfway through with our already extremely rich lunch of grilled cheeses, we decided to pack up the leftovers for dinner and substitute ice cream for the rest of our lunch calories. With bellies and hearts full to the point of pain, we hit the road…after placing a Sneaky Card on a random stranger's car and quickly ducking out of sight from whomever might have seen us.

After driving another 3 hours through the gorgeous Tennessee countryside, we drove through a depressing Memphis, TN in the dark. After crossing over the Mississippi River into Arkansas the mood dramatically, and almost instantly became more depressing. Suddenly there were obnoxious signs everywhere saying "Report Drunk Driving" and "Zero Tolerance Policy for Speeding Statewide".

I guess lots of folks from Arkansas drive over to Memphis to party, have to get themselves home somehow, and everyone just drives; no matter where their heads are at. We all agreed to keep to the strict speed limit and committed to zero talking on the phone, even though we did almost none of that anyhow. We already kinda live in the same brain, and by this time had even gotten on the same potty, gas & snack schedule.

Actually, our road snacking deserves to be mentioned at this point. Apparently it's pretty normal for healthy eaters to completely remove all standards for nutrition when faced with a road trip. Never in my whole life have I ever consumed so much garbage coffee and crap snacks! Our snackage ranged from Slim Jims, to Fritos, loads of Gatorade, Reese's Pieces, and my personal favorite, the white cheddar popcorn that became an accidental staple. We'd stop for gas and take turns in the facilities, then each of us would inevitably return from the minimart with bags of the addictive substance, claiming to not realize that someone else had already stocked up. After all, we DID have 3 humans plus 1 dog, in 2 vehicles, and never wanted to run out. I think towards the end we started expanding our palates to fruit, yogurt and trail mix, but it certainly didn't start out that way!

We stopped at an Exxon in "West Memphis", (which is *actually* in Arkansas. Just like how there's a "West New York" in New Jersey). I took advantage of the working restroom inside, where I spotted a peculiar sign. Written in sharpie on butcher paper on the back of the ladies bathroom door read; "Ladies, please STOP putting diapers in the toilet. We have small trash cans in there for that. Thanks, Mgt." I was starting to get a pretty clear picture of what Arkansas might have to offer.

Apparently while I was in the bathroom, Andrew got approached several times for drugs; making me change my mind about trying to leave a Sneaky Card on any strange cars at that stop. Neither one of us were quite certain if they were trying to buy drugs from him, or sell to him; at the time, my little bro was a pretty laid back, long haired Sierra Nevada Jesus lookin' hippie sort, so who knows? Either way, we decided not to linger or ask anyone for directions. Without human aid, we found our way to the sketchiest part of town where our next motel was waiting for us.

So there we were, checking into our second motel of the WOOF in Forrest City, Arkansas. This one had their doors all on the outside of the building, a little more typical. Andrew and I executed the plan I had devised that morning, avoiding that absurd fee by checking in as just the two of us, driving around and sneaking Amy in afterwards. It really seems petty now, but it made all the sense in the world at the time.

We signed up for the rewards program, foolishly assuming that keeping the receipt from the previous night in Virginia would give us credit for that night…we were wrong; but we signed up anyway. After all, it would be worth it eventually… right?

Parts of the building were clearly under construction at the time, so the outside was in complete disarray. We parked as close as we could to our room and unloaded ourselves. There were illegal activities clearly happening in various dark, and some not so dark corners of the place, and I was suddenly worried about all my stuff that was left in the car and U-Haul unattended! I thought for a moment about sleeping in the car in shifts…but that, of course, was sheer foolishness. Why risk bodily harm just to try and defend my "stuff?" Instead I called mom, who was finally home from Israel. Trying to suppress the panic in my voice I reported the situation and asked her to; "Please pray for protection over our stuff outside, this part of Arkansas seems to be a bit _meth-y_." My mother is a fierce mama-bear, and has an intense prayer life…so it wouldn't surprise me if she stayed up all night fulfilling my request.

This motel was quite the downgrade from Virginia. The luxurious whole bathroom in Virginia had an abundance of towels, a whole tissue box, plus back up toilet paper. In Arkansas, the bathroom situation was divided up…the toilet and shower were in one room, and the sink area was more or less a part of the bedroom. In place of a whole tissue box, there were packets of travel tissues scattered around the sink area, backup toilet paper was nowhere to be found, half the outlets didn't work, and the refrigerator was busted. But at least the microwave was in working order, _filthy_, but functional…so at least we could enjoy our warmed-up leftovers.

That night while we were settling in, worrying about my things outside, and trying to make plans for the next day, I told my traveling companions about the last time I drove through Arkansas...I was 9 years old, and on a 3 month long road trip with mom, all 3 siblings and our maternal grandparents in a 35' motorhome. My older brother, Nick and I developed a fascination with Arkansas when we got our hands on a book of archaic state laws that are technically still in place, but so outdated that they're rarely paid attention to and never enforced.

Here are the few about Arkansas we liked the most:

1. In Little Rock, men and women are not allowed to flirt in public or could face up to 30 days in jail.
2. A man may legally beat his wife, but only once a month.
3. You are not allowed to keep an alligator in a bathtub.
4. The Arkansas River may not rise higher than the Main Street Bridge in Little Rock. (Not sure exactly how one would go about enforcing this one or who would even be punished.) ...*and finally...*
5. It is prohibited to pronounce "Arkansas" incorrectly.

Now, I might never have even thought to _do_ that, but now that I know I'm not _supposed_ to, it was high time I figured *EVERY* way I could! "R-Kansas", "Arken-Sas", and "Arken's-Ass" are the only three I can remember now...probably because they're the only ones you can legitimately come up with without adding extra letters that simply aren't there to begin with.

As we polished off our leftovers from the Grilled Cheeserie,

Andrew and Amy excitedly told me how close we were going to be to Crater of Diamonds State Park! They are rock hounds and natural born treasure hunters, so they had dreamed of going there someday, and this just seemed like the time. I mean, why not? It wasn't going to be all that far out of our way, and by the time we talked it out, it sounded simply *irresponsible* not to go! ...and this is how I get talked into things.

So, after carefully mapping out this new side adventure, we hit the cards once again and then passed out. Another day well played.

12

Westward: Five Doors Later

Sunday, January 26th:

We had passed through our first time zone change the day before, so we were all up at the crack of dawn. In that early morning, all was as it should be, and after leaving a Sneaky Card in the disgusting refrigerator, we headed down to the lobby for the loveliest continental breakfast I could have hoped for in a place like that! We indulged in everything on the spot, *plus* packed in whatever we could sneak into our pockets and kept to ourselves.

At that hour the lobby was full of employees filling their bellies before work…and even though this was a "dog friendly" motel, they all seemed uneasy around my small bear, and made a point to let us know that she was NOT welcome in the carpeted, food service area. I wanted to counter them by showing them her Service Animal Card, but didn't want to make waves or get stabbed. So as usual, Pepper was the center of attention, but this time not in such a good way.

Somehow, despite our excellent taste in food, none of us were coffee snobs, but we were getting pretty tired of truck stop java, so we decided to try and find "real coffee". Using her impressive internet skills, Amy honed in on a trendy place called "Nexus Coffee" in Little Rock, Arkansas, so that would be our first real stop. We also decided it was high time we got bolder with our "Sneaky Cards", and coffee shops are ideal when it comes to awkward behavior.

Parking the U-Haul a little ways away, we had a bit of a trek to get there, and on the way we ran into a white, middle aged, dread locked, shabby, but pleasant hippie trying to sell us a painting. It was a nice painting, but since we were all on a budget, and carried almost zero cash, we had to decline the actual purchase. Not wanting to just blow him off, Andrew asked the fella what the painting was about, the man replied; "LOVE man! *Pure Love!*" And insisted that we just keep it. Andrew delightfully accepted this surprise gift and talked a bit with our new friend. I still think of that guy from time to time, especially since his little art piece is still hanging up in my room at Grandma's house. I think most folks, including myself at the time, might have just shrugged him off since we were, after all, "on a schedule, _and_ on a budget" then plowed ahead to our goal. But no, Andrew wanted to take the time to really see him, engage in brief conversation, and _then_ move along.

By the time we reached Nexus Coffee, there was a line, so we had plenty of time to conspire with whom to play our "Sneaky Cards" game. Up until now we had been silently executing the ones whose "actions" were simply leaving them in odd places to be found. Challenging one another, we were about to get interactive. Andrew chose to "High Five 4 random people, the last person you high five gets the card". Andrew, ever the charismatic goofball, had zero problem finding participants… and naturally managed to draw plenty of attention to our odd little trio plus giant dog party. Thanks to Andrew paving the way for us, Amy and I had no trouble engaging strangers in these out of the ordinary shenanigans.

My card was to "find someone taller than myself" and give them the card. At 5'4" that was pretty easy, however, I chose the tallest person I could find, making _his_ challenge even harder. Amy's card demanded she yell "MARCO!" in public, and give the card to the first person who hollers back; "POLO!"

A girl could get used to all of this free entertainment so long as you don't care too much about what random strangers might think about you. Which is easy enough when you're like 100% sure you'll never see any of those strangers, ever again.

After a brief exploration of downtown Little Rock, we were off like a herd of turtles to find Crater of Diamonds State Park! It's apparently the only place left in the world where the public can "mine" their own diamonds by hand. It had rained the night before, making it an excellent day for spotting diamonds! (I didn't know this detail about gem hunting, but my fellow gem-hunters were _well_ aware.) Clothing wise, we were completely unprepared for this adventure...but nothing can keep a Mayne from looking for treasures. Where we were strongly advised to don waterproof shoes, water-resistant pants and gloves, we had jeans, cheap rubber gardening gloves and plastic shopping bags over our sneakers held in place by rubber bands.

While we were gearing up as best we could in the parking lot, I noticed plenty of dogs locked in cars with the windows cracked. And since I wasn't exactly interested in having a mud-ball in the back seat of my car for the remainder of the trip, we decided that we'd leave our ferocious pup to guard the car & U-Haul from inside the Nissan.

Once on the muddy site, we searched and searched alongside

an adorable little family who were also on a road trip across the country. They were just as unprepared as we were, so we made each other feel a little less awkward about being there in our shabby state of dress.

We ended up finding one *super tiny* diamond after another!! With every find we would run to the person who found it, jump up and down, hug each other and howl into the air!! Our glee was contagious, and with the air practically *magnetic* with enthusiasm, we were crowded with more treasure hunters within minutes of each find.

Andrew, Amy & I each found one, then gave our fourth found diamond to the little 5 year old girl hunting with us, I'm pretty sure she and her mom both cried.

Unfortunately when we went to have them checked at the end of the day, it turned out they were all quartz...so, while the "diamonds" were "fake", the joy was *real*. And that's what matters to people like us.

Still reeling from endorphins, we hit the road in search of Texas. Don't worry, we found it...as it turns out, it's a little hard to miss. We hadn't quite decided if we were celebrating having checked off something from the Mayne's bucket list, or mourning the fact that our "diamonds" turned out to be quartz...either way, we concluded that Mexican food was in order. We found Fuzzy's Taco Shop in Texarkana, a town half in Arkansas and half in Texas. Again, Pepper was welcomed warmly with her service card, and the staff had what felt like a hundred questions, and I was happy to answer them all and make up the ones I wasn't sure about. The taco shop was just what the doctor ordered! Mexican food is our shared love language. If you're celebrating, tacos will make it more festive. If you're sad, tacos will cheer you up. When in doubt...tacos...or burritos, whatever.

So up until now our mapping had been pretty spot on timing wise. But we were about to come to a cruel reminder that Google Maps is assuming you are going the speed limit, and upon entering Texas we were catapulted into a bit of a twilight zone with the speed limit jumping from 55ish to 80 miles per hour. Suddenly our poor little U-Haul Charlotte couldn't keep up. And even if we pushed her to go above 60, it wasn't worth the dramatic change in gas mileage. She also had a "red zone" on the speedometer with an ominous statement reading: "SPEED KILLS". So now our daily arrival times to the next Red WOOF would be a little more of a guessing game. Thankfully we had the best navigator _ever_ in Amy! However, on this particular day, Amy wanted some alone time in the little car with Pepper and her music, so I drove with Andrew in the U-Haul for a spell. Now, we had been driving with the U-Haul leading the way, since it's easier to spot a giant green spider on a truck then it is a tiny red car in traffic. We kept to this habit we had fallen into, with the U-Haul in front, making _me_ Andrew's co-pilot...this resulted in us getting terribly lost since Amy was our chief navigator and she was no longer leading the way.

We finally arrived in Mesquite, Texas _way_ after our originally planned time. Again, Andrew and I checked in, leaving Amy & Pepper behind with the vehicles. This Red WOOF was more unnerving than the last. We entered into a tiny box of a room since the "main lobby" was closed after dark. The man working behind the bulletproof glass hardly looked up at us during our whole check in. Directly behind us in this tiny check in area there were vending machines with all the "extras." So now we'd gone from "We will bring you whatever you forgot, free of charge, read you a bedtime story and tuck you in." To;

"You forgot something? Too bad. It's over there, in a vending machine, you have to pay for it, and NO we don't have any change."

Once we successfully checked in, we went to fetch Amy & Pepper from the vehicles and headed up to the second floor where the doors were once again on the outside of the building. Never wanting to be dehydrated, we always arrived at a place desperately needing to use the facilities. As we piled into the room and took our turns in the loo, we discovered the bathroom door was pretty busted. It didn't close even ¾ the way, the backing was coming off, and with every attempt to close it further, the backing became more and more dislodged.

We sent Amy and Pepper back to the vehicles, (to avoid that third party detection) and I decided to go down and let the guy behind the glass know about it. I didn't care so much about privacy at this point, but I _did_ care about being charged for some sort of damage to the room that wasn't something _we_ did. So I simply needed him to make a note or something stating that the room "came that way". To my surprise, he wanted to give us another room! So up the stairs I went, back to Andrew with a key to another room. This time I didn't even put the key in the door since the drapes were wide open, all the lights were on, the bed was unmade, towels were in piles around the room and there seemed to be someone in the shower. _HARD PASS_! This time Andrew went back to talk to the guy, who decided to grab the keys to every available room and make the hike up the stairs himself.

He took a look at the unmade, obviously occupied room to make sure we weren't lying to him for some stupid reason, and led us to a third room. This one simply _REEKED_ of cigarette smoke. We can all deal with some degree of stank, but as former smokers, Andrew and Amy understandably couldn't deal with this particular odor. Rejecting that room, we moved on. Behind door number four we found yet another smoke soaked room, this one with the added touch of flickering lights above the beds…great, so this place is also haunted.

Finally, exhausted from not only this process but from the entire day, we told the guy we will just go back to room number one if he will just put a note that *WE* didn't break the bathroom door. But no, this process seemed to have sparked a fiery determination in this Texan to find an appropriate sleeping space for us. I couldn't help but think "Do you have a stable out back? I'll sleep with the livestock, that won't be so bad for one night, right?" *Finally,* at our fifth and final stop, we had no nasty surprises. The guy went back to his bullet proof box and we fetched an exhausted Amy & bored Pepper from the parking lot. Playing cards of any sort became completely out of the question, so we simply settled in and passed out.

13

Westward: da Corner of Safe & Stabby

Monday, January 27th:

We weren't surprised to find that there would be no continental breakfast like we had in Arkansas. "No frills" meant "_GET OUT as quickly as you can._" In Texas. On the hunt for food that morning, we left in dense traffic surrounded by a thick fog. We finally made it out of the Dallas area and found a delightful and spacious Starbucks in Hudson Oaks. I'd gotten so used to hole-in-the-wall places in Manhattan, that this gargantuan space seemed ominous at first. But they welcomed us warmly, including Pepper. While we were waiting for our drinks, the barista making them, pointed to Pepper and asked "can she have a puppuccino?" Having absolutely no clue what that meant, _of course_ I said yes. Much to everyone's delight, this was simply a small cup of lightly sweetened whipped cream! Great, now Pepper has a new favorite treat.

After all the excitement of the previous day, it was nice to have a serious driving day. No special stops, no adventures, just drive. Maybe this had a little to do with the fact that there's almost nothing between Dallas and El Paso.

At one of our many potty, gas & snack stops it was brought to my attention that it was the 27th! Amy & Andrew had gotten married on April 27th the previous year, and had made the conscious decision to celebrate their "anniversary" on the 27th of each month for the first year of their marriage. Those two are so cute, that it touches me deep down…in my gag reflex.

We agreed to check into our room as quickly as humanly possible to facilitate date night. Battling the clock using Google Maps, we were going to arrive so late they would only have time to grab a simple dinner of sushi at this place Amy remembered liking on a previous trip. However, upon *actual* arrival, our clocks turned back 1 hour! We had *all* forgotten about the time change which happened moments before hitting El Paso.

We found our next motel of the WOOF on the corner of Safe & Stabby, so I left Andrew with Amy to protect our caravan while I checked us in. I approached the front desk, all excited to cash in on our free night after paying for 2 using the rewards program! The person manning the desk couldn't have been more useless when it came to this request. He had no idea what I was talking about, and I didn't see any of those convenient signs anywhere boasting of the company wide slogan of; "Stay Two Nights Get One FREE!!" He asked a fellow co-worker about it and that person awkwardly told me that there was some sort of deal associated with the points I've been acquiring, and they could only be redeemed by using the online reservation system. The way she explained it made little sense to me, so I decided to just suck it up and pay for the room up front; after all, I had to get those crazy kids off on their date!

Before leaving however, Andrew hit the bathroom in our room, and he had to clean it. A lot. He kept the gruesome details of this cleanup to himself until the next day after we left, not wanting to be forced into changing rooms like in Mesquite, thus delaying date night. I mostly remember him using grand gestures and colorful words to describe the "brownishness" he had cleaned before anyone else took a turn in that bathroom.

After they were finally on their way to dinner, I thought it would be nice to have a soak in a hot bath…that's when I noticed the long brown hairs which clung to the off white, black & brown marble shower walls. Gross, but not completely unsanitary, I washed them away, and tried to forget about it. Next I ran the faucet for what should have been hot water. For like 20 minutes. After which time, the water was still icy cold and not showing any signs of improvement…I accepted the fact that a hot bath was going to be out of the question, and even a simple shower wouldn't be on the menu until the next night. If I had more energy, less stuff to move, and maybe not a giant canine in tow, I might have asked to switch rooms. But the truth of the matter was that I simply couldn't be bothered to care about creature comforts anymore that day.

Next, I decided to call customer service to figure out this whole business with the points, and see about our free room which was feeling more and more unlikely by that time. The pleasant guy on the phone informed me that my points would reflect on my account 10-14 days after my stay and may be redeemed for future stays. So; "stay 2 nights get 1 night free" was not meant to be taken literally or in a linear fashion. More like; "The points you acquire today may someday earn you a free night with us. Somewhere else. Enjoy *that* place." This is the restaurant equivalent of; "buy 2 entrees, get one free! But not for 2 weeks." I didn't even have the energy to be upset about it, and the customer service representative was kind enough to help me book our next night in advance. For some reason I overshared and admitted we were a pack of 3 humans and a dog, so that absurd $7 fee we'd been so sneakily avoiding was back in play, adding just another annoyance to an already frustrating evening.

I decided to at least pretend to be asleep before Amy & Andrew returned from their date...foul moods are contagious, and I didn't want to infect them with mine. I finally drifted peacefully off to sleep with some variation of a "let it go" mantra playing on a loop in my head.

14

Westward: Praise The Lard!

Tuesday, January 28th:

We left the next morning without mentioning to the staff _everything_ that was wrong with our foul bathroom. I was pretty sure they knew how bad their motel was, probably didn't care, and I didn't feel like starting out _my_ day with a complaint.

We had enjoyed our Starbucks breakfast the day before so much that we decided to go for it again. Pepper, of course, was offered another puppuccino and was decidedly the center of everyone's attention. The place was on the smaller side (for Texas) and we sat next to some colorful local gents who were sharing their homemade brownies with everyone present. We made certain of course that these weren't "special" brownies before we accepted their invitation to partake. Lord only knows we didn't wanna get stuck for another night in El Paso simply because we accidentally ingested more than we bargained for! We stayed awhile, swapped gem hunting stories, and one guy went on and on about various places where he'd hunted down local semi-precious stones...leaving us wanting to come back in search of their hidden locations. Next time Texas, next time.

Back on the road again, we set ourselves up for a long day of boring driving...there isn't much between El Paso, TX and Blythe, CA. Sorry Arizona & New Mexico, I'm sure you both have some lovely qualities out there somewhere, but since they're not along highway 10, we didn't have time to find them.

However, after less than an hour on the road, we came across a spectacle we simply couldn't pass up. It was Bowlin's Akela Flats in New Mexico. It was a single shop, but it's facade was painted to look like the downtown strip of an old western town. Inside we discovered an enormous tourist trap! Signs everywhere boasted; "Fireworks Sold Year Round!" "Native Art!" "Fine Jewelry!" & "Western Wear!" We found some more or less authentic items...mostly "less."

Andrew nearly cried when he saw a fireworks package much taller and wider than himself, and with a price tag of $700 it was easy for him to hold back in purchasing it. I would remind him of this excitement over these fireworks a mere 18 months later when his infant son was trying to sleep, and he reported our neighbors for setting off fireworks in the neighborhood.

Amy purchased a nightlight with a beautifully hand painted hummingbird on a slice of thin transparent stone, and I refrained from walking away with a tin of "Alien Poop Mints." Andrew and I couldn't leave completely empty handed though, so we got some "party snaps", a tiny little firecracker, completely legal in California.

Back on the road again, we started seeing signs for an intriguing spot; Dwayne's Jerky Shop in Bowie, AZ. We were raised in homes where dad hunted, most of our meat came from the wild, and jerky was a staple for preservation. So naturally we _had_ to stop, and I'm glad we did! Not only did they have jerky from a wide range of animals including sharks, they also offered local honey and a huge selection of treats made from prickly pear, which is one of the fruits born from a particular cactus. So we had planned on a boring day of driving, but instead, ended up finding some fascinating & delicious treats!

Next we drove right through a small town called Quartzite in Arizona, 25 minutes from the border of California. Quartzite holds a special place in my heart since my grandparents took me there several times as a young adult for the gem & RV show. Given their aforementioned "rock hound" status, Andrew and Amy had always wanted to attend the show and never got the chance...unfortunately this would not be the time, since we had already veered off course searching for diamonds in Arkansas, and according to U-Haul rules, we had to get the truck back within a certain time frame, under a specific mileage, and we were already pushing it. So, for now, exploring the show would have to remain a goal set for the future.

When we crossed over from Arizona to California we hit border patrol. I had no idea that was a thing between our states, but I guess being so close to Mexico, they feel the need to check. Andrew got stuck for a while since they wanted to _really_ check the U-haul for stowaways. After clearing him, the border patrol gave him a piece of paper indicating that he'd been cleared. A few miles down the road we noticed that the price of gas went up a whole dollar! Oh well, it was simply too late to turn around and go through border patrol again just to save a few bucks.

We cruised into our next motel of the WOOF with high hopes. Not exactly sure why, but hey, we're optimists! Upon checking in, the woman insisted that we booked a room with a single king sized bed. I was even more insistent that no, we would never have done such a thing, since we are three adults, not interested in co-sleeping. She reluctantly gave in and found us a proper room with 2 queens. When we got to our room, we discovered that the place was severely lacking in amenities. The room was booked for three, with towels for one and no soap of any kind. Not the end of the world by a long shot, and after the downward spiral we'd been experiencing with this particular chain, our expectations hit an all time low. We were not shocked, and didn't care anymore about correcting the problem. This would prove to be another night of simply giving up on the idea of a shower. Besides, we would be at grandma's the next day, where clean towels, every cleanser imaginable and all the hot water you could ever hope for would be available in abundance.

Thankfully we had gotten into town with plenty of time to find a place to eat a proper meal, which for our crew, in the southwest of this country meant, yet again, seeking out some version of Mexican food. Amy did her internet research, and found an "authentic" place within walking distance. With the gem & RV show happening that week, the town was alive! Walking to our chosen destination we passed plenty of restaurants that looked like fun, but we were determined to get to the "authentic" Mexican restaurant we had chosen.

Approaching the restaurant, the place practically looked closed. The wooden shades leftover from the 1970s were drawn, and when we walked in, it was clear that the place hadn't seen an upgrade in style for at least as long as the shades had been there. A dilapidated podium where maybe a greeter once stood, blocked our pathway inside, the ceilings were low, and not in a sexy way. The entire restaurant had short, burgundy carpet speckled with stains & cigarette burns. There was a waiting area furnished with a few mismatched, floral printed shabby couches, a crumbling coffee table scattered with worn out magazines, and old stained glass lamps lit the place poorly.

Smells are very important to a dining atmosphere, and this place was a combination of "moldy basement," "grandma's haunted attic" and "greasy restaurant that hadn't been cleaned in a few decades". If everything had been maintained well, the place might have been considered "vintage" or even "trendy", but no. It was clearly just old and gross. The dining area was a ghost town, and the couple sitting at the bar drinking their dinner only made the place look even sadder and more out of time in this spunky little town.

The woman working behind the bar came to "greet" us with a look on her face that screamed "I've just had a rotten day, probably a lousy life, and you just made it worse by walking in that door." She _really_ didn't want to accept Pepper's Service Animal status…but, having no choice, she reluctantly sat us in a booth patched together with gray duct tape. After tossing the menus in the center of the table, she blurted out; "Everything we serve here is cooked in lard! Just so you know." To which Andrew replied without _any_ hesitation, "Oh great! We _LOVE_ lard!!" Her face went from startled to perplexed to disgusted in a few short moments, right before she darted back behind the bar.

We peeled the menus off the sticky table top, looked over the options, and decided not to stay. Honestly, the menu items looked acceptable, but the atmosphere, combined with our server's attitude didn't bode well for our having a good time. So we retraced our steps back to a lively BBQ joint we had passed on our way which boasted of a "Taco Tuesday" night. This turned out to be the best decision of our whole day! The place was being run mostly by a bunch of white teenage girls and Mexican boys…just sayin', the place was lively, enthusiastic, clean and had killer food. We chose to sit outside, where everyone we came in contact with treated all of us like celebrities, especially Pepper! And after asking our permission, they even brought her multiple giant treats and plenty of water.

Halfway through our meal, we described what had happened to us at the "authentic" Mexican restaurant where we started out that evening. The girl waiting on us started laughing so hard I thought she might pee herself! Apparently she lives with her aunt, and that was the woman who treated us so poorly… they're constantly at odds with each other, and now she's got ammo….oops.

We went back to the motel and filled the rest of our evening playing cards and trying out the various snacks we had picked up from the jerky shop. We also took an inventory of our "driving food", knowing we would want to consume & destroy any evidence of the crap snacks we had acquired during our journey…we were about to be landing at grandma's house, where the only things on the approved menu had to be "good for you." Besides, our insides weren't exactly thrilled with our eating habits during the trip, and we all vowed to start eating healthier once we arrived back home.

15

Westward: Chasing The Final Sunset

Wednesday, January 29th:

Crossing so many time zones one day at a time, Andrew and I woke up at the crack of 4:00 am. We decided to let Amy sleep and head back across the border of Arizona for that sweet, sweet cheap gas. Teetering on the edge of the time zone change, the clock on my phone kept bouncing back & forth on me, so I had no idea what time it really was by the time we got back to border patrol. I only know that it was dark, and the stars were still showing off. Andrew and I hunkered down, and prepared for another cavity search of the U-Haul, and were pleasantly surprised when the paper he had received from the day before gave us a free pass! Like, how easy would it have been to get that paper, spend the night in California, drive back over, pick up a bunch of "new friends" and hop back over? This can be a strange country.

Amy was awake and mostly packed by the time we returned with breakfast, so we got a nice, early start. We decided to drive through Joshua Tree National Park. It wasn't that far out of our way, and after a few days of driving through Texas, we felt we deserved an upgrade in scenery. U-Haul mileage be damned!

Cruising into the park, it was way too early, and the ranger station wasn't even open yet, so we had to rely on our phones to direct us around. We found some blooming cacti, a fun little grove of palm trees, and more than one giant rock to climb. Around mid-morning, we encountered some European tourists and took turns taking photos for each other…this is the only reason I even have pictures of the three of us from that trip!

By the time we exited the park, the ranger station was open and they wanted us to pay for our cars. As usual, Andrew was leading the way with the U-Haul…to this day I have no idea what exactly Andrew said to them, but after a brief chat, Andrew used his "Andrew skills" and we only had to pay for one of our vehicles.

We weren't used to getting so much exercise on the road, so we were all famished by the time we left the park…it was time to find more food. We happened upon a coffee shop in the middle of nowhere, went in, ordered and paid. The establishment looked like they had plucked it from a posh urban area and plopped it in the middle of the desert. It had industrial concrete floors, a multitude of fancy pastries, all the trending espresso drinks, a section devoted to tee shirts and various trinkets, and none of the wooden tables & chairs matched…but in a way that made it clear that it had been designed that way on purpose. The two hipsters working there seemed to be in their early 30s, and were complete with beards and "man-buns". And they worked quickly, leading me to believe that perhaps they were the owners and not your typical lazy, coffee shop employees.

I told 'man-bun 1" that I was going to get my service dog from the car, to which he boldly asked me; "what service does she provide?" Not having been asked that question the whole trip,

I hesitated, then, without waiting for me to respond, he smugly stated; "because we don't accept emotional support animals here." Had I been more prepared I might have put her jacket on and told him that she's my hiking dog, carrying my stuff since I have a bad back. (That *is* how she's registered by the way.) But, I was not prepared for such a blunt attack, so we ended up sitting outside in the freezing desert wind with our dangerous creature, chowing down and getting on our way as quickly as we could.

The remaining 7 hour drive to Copperopolis was as uneventful as we expected, driving up highway 99 in the middle of California isn't as glamorous as one might think, unless you're from California, in which case you already know how exotic 99 *isn't*.

We arrived home well after dark, dirty & exhausted but happy. And we couldn't *wait* to pamper ourselves with all of the amenities that came with grandma's house. Mom had returned from her trip to Israel and made the trek from her home in Lake Tahoe to Grandma's house in Copperopolis, so she was also there waiting for us; and *finally*, we were *all* relieved *NOT* to be checking into yet another Red WOOF.

For the record, yes…I did end up racking up points for each of those wretched motel stays, but it took an entire year, and many hours of therapy before I was brave enough to stay the night in one of those "Red WOOF" motels again…however, *that* is a story for another time.

16

Rough Landing

The second day after I moved in with my grandma in February of 2020, I walked into the garage to find grandma and my mother having a heated discussion. I of course tried to back out without being noticed, but it was too late! I had been spotted; therefore put on the spot and dragged into a discussion that apparently included me. Suddenly I felt like judge and jury.

Grandma: "Well, I was just explaining to your _mother_ that now, since you're here, I want to send back my "*fall bracelet" and stop spending all that money! (She hated spending money on something that might never be used for its intended purpose.)"

Mom: "And I was just explaining to _her_ that she has to _promise_ not to climb any trees if she sends it back! Having you here doesn't suddenly give her license to keep climbing trees!"

Grandma finally agreed to stay out of the trees, and allow me to exercise my finest MonkeyDancerGoat skills during harvest season; and then of course pruning. We did after all have three trees including figs, pomegranates and persimmons that would all require these climbing skills

I couldn't help but laugh…I mean, if *that* was as bad as fighting got around here, everything was going to be just fine. So the next day grandma called up the company to cancel her device and gathered all the hardware together to send it back. She only had the gear for 3 years, the woman never threw anything away, so naturally she still had the original box and knew exactly where it was. The look of satisfaction on her face when she dropped it at the UPS store was priceless…she was practically giddy.

The next night, she and I were playing cards. She had been widowed for a little over 2 years by that time, and I had just left a wretched roommate situation after being divorced…therefore, we were both just *so* happy to finally have each other, that we would stay up way too late playing cards almost every night in those first few months!

At 11:15 pm the phone rang, and it was the landline. (For those of you who may not understand this, it is a phone designated to the house, also connected to the house in question, and not a person…some people still had these in 2020.) We exchanged surprised looks, I panicked inside ever so slightly, since a call that late at night is rarely good news. Suspiciously I picked up the phone; it was an automated voice…something about a fall. Then grandma's cell phone rang, it was out next door neighbor! She got the automated call too! Moments later, yet another neighbor just showed up at the front door! I had no idea, but the way these fall bracelets work, is when they get set off, it sends the system a message to call the people on your designated list, and that list is usually your neighbors.

I had planned on meeting all the neighbors, just not in this fashion…with confusion and panic in the air…at 11:15 at night; them thinking grandma had fallen. So apparently when you cancel your subscription to these things, it doesn't go through until they receive the hardware back. And we had somehow failed to turn the confounded device off! Therefore, someone, somewhere within the UPS system had dropped the package, setting off the alarm and giving me the pleasure of meeting all the neighbors, the awkward way.

*Fall Bracelet;

A fall detection bracelet is a small wearable device that monitors your activity levels and alerts caregivers if you have fallen.

17

What 90#s of Hazel Can do to My Day

A few months after I moved in with my 82 year old grandmother Hazel, I came home from grocery shopping with a vague outline for my afternoon. Yoga, writing, grooming my dog, maybe reorganizing the freezer or making a new spreadsheet for something mundane; the plague had been going on for about 3 months, and life was still weird, but we were starting to get a handle on things again.

I went to check on grandma with the intention of updating her on my plans for the day. She was almost always in the garden that time of year, and on my way to the backyard I noticed that she had put a couple of lamb chops on the deck upstairs to defrost in the sun…I couldn't help but think; *"maybe they should be covered, but whatever, I'm sure she knows what she's doing."*

I walked down the stairs to the backyard overlooking the lake only to find Hazel trying to operate a chainsaw…on a stick! Well, my afternoon was about to change. I learned that this deadly weapon was called a "pole saw", and proceeded to try and figure out how to use it. We quickly discovered that while this may be a one person job for an average sized dude, it's a two person job when one of them is a 90 lb, 4'10 82 year old workhorse and the other person is me. We both decided that I would manage the sharp end, and she would manage the on/off switch, all the way at the bottom of the stick. Naturally we also had to be connected to power, so then we had the added fun of dragging around an extension cord that is obviously trying to kill us both.

At one point during all of this I looked down and realized that I hadn't changed out of my flip flops, *"I should probably put on some protective footwear"* I thought, but then thought *"nah, this won't take long right? And I'm super careful. Besides, if I walk away right now, even for a few minutes, grandma might try and do this on her own."*

We then proceeded to cut away branches, stumps, roots etc. all while navigating the obstacle course that is the yard, complete with multiple flights of stairs, uneven terrain and a 100 lb Bernese Mountain Dog named Pepper. To make things even more frustrating was the fact that grandma is a bit hard of hearing. They say communication is key, and in this case <u>our</u> communication was bogged down by chainsaw racket, one party who can't hear very well, and a miscommunication could possibly result in the misfire of a very dangerous power tool; I'd grown attached to most of my extremities by this point in my life and injuring any of them could really put a damper on my week. We managed to get through the projects on her agenda without casualties despite the fact that we were laughing almost the entire time.

When we finally got finished, I went back upstairs only to find one of the lamb chops was <u>gone</u>. I really try not to panic in these situations, but the bone in this thing is shaped like an uppercase T, and if Pepper, true to Mountain Dog form, had decided to swallow it in a single gulp, we could be looking at a life threatening blockage. She'd already had one major, life saving surgery in her golden years, and there was no way I would subject her to anesthesia & recovery again. I got my mom on the phone, pray. Just pray. Tell everyone you know to pray. I don't care what they believe, or who they go to in times of need, just ask them to pray! I called the vet, and she instructed me to feed Pepper as much as she was willing to eat. The reason for this (if she swallowed it) would be to pad her intestines as much as possible for the passage of the bone. Bread, she told me. We needed _lots_ of bread.

The vet on the phone told me that I was lucky, since Bernese are quite well known for being a bottomless pit when it comes to food! This was when I learned that Pepper was a bread snob. We have a constant stream of company (usually well over 100 visitors) from May - September, and 99% of the food left behind ends up in the freezer for future use. We had dinner rolls that had been there since Thanksgiving 6 years ago, gluten free hamburger buns from whenever that was trendy; potato bread for some reason, whole wheat for when grilled cheeses were on the kids menu, and even some sort of pita situation. It was all fair game. I began defrosting and Pepper began the feasting.

By now Pepper was happy as a clam. (*How we know clams are actually happy is beyond my expertise, but who am I to question these things?*) She went through almost all of the bread selection, but by the time we got to the dinner rolls she turned up her nose and simply refused to keep eating. I suddenly remembered that olive oil is good for dogs, so I grabbed some and began soaking the dry, flavorless lumps in the oil. That did the trick, she ate them right up! I couldn't help but think; *"I can't believe I'm soaking bread in olive oil....for a dog!"* I went to the store for backup bread and canned pumpkin which is a natural doggie laxative if needed. For the next few days I had the extra fun job of squishing through all of her excrement checking for bone bits; evidence that she had actually been the culprit of the missing lamb chop. But that process proved nothing....she never missed a beat and I found zero bone bits.

We've come up with several theories as to what actually happened. Maybe since the lamb chop was raw, her stomach acids dissolved the bone as would a wolf's. (They *are* designed to eat raw flesh and sometimes eat bones). Maybe it was all those prayers and a miracle occurred (Wahoo!). And in the final scenario she's 100% innocent in the theft. She's never been one to take people food even when left alone with it. I once had a roommate make a breakfast sandwich, put it on the coffee table, go take a shower, and return to find her just *staring* at it. (Which makes me think; *"who makes a breakfast sandwich of all things, then goes and takes a 20 minute shower, leaving the eggs to rubberize and cheese to get all "not awesome"? What a weirdo."*) So it is entirely reasonable to think it was taken by a bird of prey. We have *plenty* of giant raptors here, and I wouldn't put it past any of them to make off with a 6 oz lamb chop. Whatever happened, we will never be able to prove anything either way, and I still don't know what to do with all that canned pumpkin.

18

Sweet Dreams Are Made of Peas

I have been an enthusiastic gardener for as long as I can remember. My paternal grandparents, who lived in the Oakland Hills of California were my inspiration…but they lived in a magical microclimate that could grow just about anything; and I lived in the chilly Sierra Nevada Mountains of Lake Tahoe. The climate never discouraged me though, I was determined to grow things! When I was 12, I got my first "paycheck" job at a local nursery called The Watermelon Patch. It was there that I learned all about what was possible to grow in this high altitude, snow heavy, short growing season of a place. Refusing to be discouraged, I planted everything I thought "just might make it."

When I left home at 18 to pursue my ballet career, I lived in dodgy places around New Orleans, the slums of Philadelphia, divey parts of San Francisco and then midtown Manhattan. Over those years my gardening passions were put on the back burner since there were never any acceptable outdoor spaces. So, in my late 20s, when I moved to Hoboken, New Jersey and suddenly had a private back yard, I was back at it full force!

Growing in New Jersey is amazing! There's a reason they call it "The Garden State." Naturally I overdid it, and the first season I ended up with more veggies than I could handle...but hey, that's why we have pickle recipes right? After I moved from my condo with the private back yard to a 2 bedroom apartment above the bar I had just opened, I joined the community garden. Again, I went overboard every year. The last plot I managed was an all out jungle by September with basil as tall as myself.

Naturally, when I moved to Lake Tulloch, CA in 2020 I was thrilled at the idea of growing in a different climate! I have since learned that hotter doesn't always mean better, especially with finicky vegetables. We also don't have a fence to keep the deer at bay, and we have birds. Lots and lots of birds....and even though everyone at the house enjoys watching them, birds are notorious thieves.

That first year I tried lots of things that failed, but even more that worked! To my great disappointment, peas were on the list of things that failed miserably...maybe because I tried a method I had read in a "Gardening for Seniors" book, but more likely that I took that great idea, did my own thing and never actually followed through to the end of the instructions. To this day, I couldn't tell you with any certainty whether they were under-watered, plucked out of the dirt by birds, or sprouted and grazed on by deer before I could notice them...in any case, they failed. Peas are a household favorite, so in 2021 I decided to try again... this time planting them in 3 different locations in the fenced in deer free zones, watching them like a hawk and watering obsessively. For whatever reason, to my delight, they succeeded! And by the time they started coming in, it was at just the right rate for 2 or 3 people to snack on them daily at their leisure. So you can imagine my shock when I came home to find them...*ALL. Torn. Out.*

There was a giant garbage bag of wilting plants just sitting in the garage waiting for a run to the dump. My brother Andrew was there, acting like he wandered into the room by accident, and I demanded to know what happened!! "You were supposed to be watching her!" I shouted. At that moment Grandma came around the corner, claiming full responsibility and acting a little smug about it too.

Slamming my coffee cup on the table, I exclaimed: "But why?? Why would you do that?!?" She hesitated ever so slightly and replied calmly; "Well, I was through with them. I had enough and now I'm finished." I wanted to laugh, cry, shake her and storm off all at once, so I did nothing. At which point her lower lip began to quiver a tiny bit; "I'm sorry." She muttered to herself...but also to the sack of sad discarded plants, sitting there slowly dying, still with tiny, half formed peas attached....

...And then I woke up.

19

There Be Dragons!

I live most of my kitchen life with a low grade anxiety that I'm putting the wrong thing down the garbage disposal. For whatever reason, every household that has one, has created a specific list of "no no's" which drastically differ from place to place. These unwritten lists also seem to be subject to change based on personal kitchen traumas.

So, in the places where I prepare food, the disposals have earned themselves nicknames with actual labels stuck on them, ranging from "sink dragon" to "sink demon" to "sink gecko".

The most complicated disposal situation I deal with on a daily basis is at my grandma's house. She has 2 sinks in her kitchen, each with its own "sink dragon". The dragon in the main sink gets used on a daily basis, and the other one is in the kitchen island where we almost never ask him to do much of anything.

Both are the same brand, but like most siblings, they handle things quite a bit differently from one another. Maybe it's due to how they are treated, how often they eat, or how much water they're given.

I however, like to think they simply have unique personalities. Whatever the reason, their differences make my kitchen life a tiny bit unpredictable.

A few months after moving in with grandma in 2020, I decided to make my famous asparagus/pistachio spread. It was one of my favorite things to serve with burrata cheese at the restaurant I owned in a former life of mine in New Jersey. Asparagus had come into season, thus on sale. So when it got down to $.99/lb I got almost 20 lbs. I still also had a ridiculous amount of pistachios stashed away like a squirrel, and needed to use them before they walked away on their own.

I got the kitchen all set up, dug my restaurant grade food processor out of storage, started the salted water boiling on the stove, and lined up all the other ingredients restaurant style to get it all done in one afternoon.

Making an effort to clean up after myself as I went along, I got the asparagus into the boiling water, then started feeding the trimmed asparagus ends to the sink dragon in the kitchen island. It quickly became clear that I had chosen the wrong dragon.

The backing up started, and with grandma hovering about, there was absolutely no way to let it go and address it later! I made a mad dash for the toilet plunger, and while using it to coax the mixture along, I began to notice water dripping on my feet…it was coming from the pipe under the sink where grandma kept an absurd amount of leftover liquor from days gone by. My grandparents never drank, so I can only assume it's all been left behind from one visitor or another over the past 30 years.

So there we were, I had the asparagus in salted hot water on the stove, mid-project, couldn't stop, and all of the sudden I had dirty water asparagus sludge oozing all over the hibernating booze and onto the floor.

After we pulled every bottle out so we could properly see the problem, grandma proceeded to fetch a drain snake from the neighbor's garage. *Neighbor in tow*. Now Emmit is an old fashioned neighbor with a big heart and *lots of time*. So now at this point I had a couple of 82 year olds playing plumber, in slow motion while I'm dancing around them trying to finish my project like an idiot.

After Emmit got the pipes cleared out, he noted *out loud* that there had been several clumps of egg shells lodged down there too, but not to worry, they're all cleaned out now...*geeze*! I wish he'd kept that *tiny* detail to himself!

My project turned out beautifully, the cabinet got a deep clean, bottles all polished and put away, and no, now we aren't allowed to feed egg shells to *either* sink dragon anymore. And rejected asparagus bits now get the freezer treatment in preparation to be elevated into soup form.

It seems unfair to judge the sink dragons the same, but no, the island creature had to ruin it for everyone. Unfortunately, for him, I was forced to whip out the 'ole label maker and adjust his title to reflect his demotion from "sink dragon" to "sink gecko".

Deep down I still believe that both can handle controversial things like asparagus, egg shells and more, but grandma, now traumatized by the ancient eggshells involved in the asparagus episode, has put egg shells on the "do not feed the dragons" list. Oh well, it is *her* house, they are *her* dragons, and for now she makes the rules where their menu is concerned.

My mother on the other hand, just thinks nothing can ever

get the best of her Lake Tahoe sink demon. He can handle anything!! Coffee grounds, egg shells, bones, banana peels, broccoli stems, you name it! Gluttonous behavior is typically frowned upon in most societies, but when it comes to a sink demon, gluttony is a trait to be encouraged and praised.

He's only had 3 hang ups his entire existence. His first was when an alarming amount of store bought salsa went down. I mean, we're talking long shelf life, don't understand how it's even being preserved, bunker sized tomato sludge from hell. That episode warranted a full on plumber, someone my family would _never_ call unless everyone in the family had broken appendages and the dog had eaten the plunger.

The second time was at Christmas. I was about to start feeding it some innocent veggie bits, turned it on, and was greeted by a horrifying sound that sent chills down my spine. It turned out to be a turkey neck! The bone got shoved down there with plans to turn on the sink demon to crush it to death, but being as most of my family has some level of *ADHS, the person who shoved the bone down there must have gotten sidetracked, so it just sat in wait for the next guilty bystander. Thankfully that was a quick fix, as we simply had to fish out the mangled bone and move on.

The third time was when my extended family of 18 were in town for a 4 day visit in the winter. A few days before everyone was to arrive my mom did a mom thing that blew out the power in half of the upstairs playroom & bathroom. Placing a camping lantern in the bathroom worked well enough for most bathroom activities, but unless you wanted to practice what it felt like to shower blind, you might need to shower elsewhere.

We also had to blow up 3 air mattresses to be placed in the playroom upstairs every night to accommodate our tribe, which became a comedy of errors…we would blow them up in other places in the house with power, and then move them to their intended destinations, not accounting for mismeasured spaces, furniture that had been moved during the day to make room for various games, and a 100 lb Bernese Mountain Dog who must have thought everything was a game just for her.

And don't get me started on my brother's nocturnal breathing machine…he survived, just not sure how.

As if losing power in selective parts of the house wasn't enough, two days into the four day visit, the microwave died. Completely. What could possibly break down next? Yup, you guessed it, the sink demon.

Nobody knows what he was being force fed, but he had had enough of it! The sink started backing up and my 5'1" mother (who had also apparently "had enough") grabbed the plunger from the garage and began exorcising the hole in the sink shouting "*IN JESUS' NAME*!!!!" This image is burned into my mind forever now, and to this day it's one of the most ridiculous things I've ever seen! But it worked and I'll remember it forever.

Somehow though, in spite of these supposed "traumas" at my parent's house, the sink demon menu remains unchanged…"If it fits, you can try it!…in Jesus' name."

P.S.

About 6 months after I wrote this story, grandma accidentally slayed one of her dragons. With pomegranate shells.

For those of you who might want to make the super yummy:
ASPARAGUS SPREAD

INGREDIENTS:

1 lb asparagus, trimmed and cut into 2-inch segments, or whatever your food processor can handle.

2 cloves of garlic. Unless you're a vampire, then use shallots. Or if you're more closely related to me, then use 3-4 cloves of garlic.

1 cup pistachios. Shells removed for maximum comfort.

¼ cup olive or avocado oil, or more if you like.

¾ cup grated Parmesan cheese...amount is really negotiable, as should any cheese ingredient be.

The juice from one lemon...but seriously, have you seen the variety of lemon sizes out there? The ones in my neighborhood range from golf balls to baseballs! Be smart. If you like lemon, add a lot. If you're shy about them, then maybe the tiniest amount is good for you.

Fresh ground black pepper & salt to taste. Be careful, as the asparagus is already salted, as might be the pistachios, and Parmesan, when made in the classic fashion, is also salty... you've been warned. And this is coming from a lover of salt.

DIRECTIONS:

1: Bring a large pot of water to a boil and salt it. Add the asparagus and cook it until soft but not to the point of "baby food smoosh". (8-10 min) Drain well, but keep some of that weird tasting, salted asparagus water.

2: Toss all of the solids into a food processor with 2 Tablespoons of the oil, & some of the weird water you just made. Process for as long as you like. Add more oil & weird water as needed. You decide.

NOTE: Some of you may like it chunky, some like it smooth! I for one had fun with making a chunky one in the food processor and then putting some into the Vitamix for a smoother, silkier experience. Both are fine. Just a matter of preference! Save the salt, pepper and lemon juice for the end, seasoning to taste.

*ADHS; *Attention Deficit Hyperactive "Situation". We don't believe it's a disorder, to us it's quite normal and adds to our lovability, creativity and tendency to adapt quickly.

20

Critters On Ice

There once was a man who inherited a parrot from his uncle who passed away. This uncle was a little on the rough side, and his parrot cursed like a sailor! Unable to change the parrot's potty-mouth, the man thought maybe he could scare the bird into submission by putting him in the freezer for a few minutes. He did so, and when the bird came out he apologized! Stating; "Good sir, I am so sorry for my behavior, and I swear from this moment forward I shall only speak with kindness and respect." Shocked, the man accepted this apology and began to move on with his day, only to be asked a follow up question by the winged critter: "excuse me, but may I ask...what did the chicken do?"

BUTTERCLUCK FARM:
My friend Michele in New Jersey has dogs. Big dogs. Sometimes as many as a dozen, but usually around 8 or 9...most of them weighing well over 100 lbs. Don't worry, she also has a farm in which to contain them, complete with about a hundred chickens, a sprinkling of outdoor cats, a koi pond with massive

fishes and three cows. The dogs, 2 Tibetan Mastiffs and the rest Bernese Mountain Dogs, are her family, plain and simple. They roam together, eat together and sometimes even sleep together. They are a pack.

The chickens I understand, because eggs are delicious and you can sell them. I didn't grow up with cats, so I've never been much of a cat person, but on a farm I know that they serve the purpose of controlling the rat population. The koi pond is my favorite place to have my morning coffee and chill, since it has a charming little waterfall and the fish attack the surface in mesmerizing fashion every time they are fed.

The intention behind the cows however, is a mystery to me. They aren't meat animals, and they aren't currently milking. Even if they were producing milk, I don't think they could ever produce the right amount for me to want to keep three of them all by myself. Maybe she has them to produce that unique "farm stank", or maybe it's so she's not that "crazy dog lady", that "crazy chicken lady" or that "crazy cat lady"….once you add cows, you have a _farm_!

One day in late spring, one of her giant canines died quite naturally of old age. Michele is also a surgeon, and as a doctor has a very practical view on death. Death is a part of life, and we all knew this particular four legged creature was in her final few months. As a relatively fit woman living alone (at least with no other humans) on a mini-farm in her early 50s, Michele occasionally employs a neighbor to help with the heavy lifting. This was one of those times. She called him up to come over and dig the grave… after he had dug a hole deep and wide enough for the mass of fur and limbs…down she went. After saying a few words, we began raining dirt back down over the final resting place, when suddenly Michele hollers out "OH! Hang on a sec! I've got a cat in the freezer!"

TAHOE HOUSE

My parents still live in Lake Tahoe where I grew up. They started building the house in 1977 and have added on to it a couple of times. As a child, this made for some wonky places for domesticated critters to hide when they escaped their cages. (Yes, we were still allowed to call them "cages in the '80s.) I'm pretty sure they still have some mummified hamsters accidentally stashed in more than one random wall space like stale dinner rolls. We haven't had hamsters since the early 90s, and with no dog in the house, chipmunks are the new occasional "wall residents." My parents have had to cut through various parts of drywall more than once to release them from the places they find to hide & build their nests...or go to die, depending on the season. It causes quite a disruption when they make themselves at home, especially at night when you can hear them rustling in the attic.

Now that all 4 of us kids are out of the house, and my father is most often at his shop an hour away, my mother sometimes invites small groups of friends to use the home for retreats.

One afternoon in late fall, mom was getting the house ready for a small cluster of ladies who would be retreating the next week. She was going from room to room tidying and cleaning, all while being stalked by a stealthy chipmunk! Knowing that this little guy's pop-up presence and wall scurrying might startle her guests, she decided to make an effort to catch it! It took a few days, but the thing finally ended up in one of those humane traps that my dad has had around since the 1970s. Come to think of it, my dad inherited that trap from _his_ parents, and as avid scavengers and flea market hagglers, who knows where _they_ got it from, so that contraption may have been used to catch small dinosaurs at some point.

Anyways, mom caught him alive, wanted him gone, but didn't have the heart to kill him or take the time for relocation, so she asked my dad to "take care of it". He agreed, and my mother took off for the afternoon, putting it completely out of her mind. A few days later mom went to get something out of the chest freezer in the garage, and there he was! Trap and all. So I guess "taking care of it" is open to interpretation.

SKYLINE BLVD

My paternal grandmother passed away in 2015. She and my grandfather lived most of their lives in the Oakland Hills of California.

Their 2 acres of property was desolate when they first bought it in 1955, but with decades of tender loving care, they developed it into quite the gardener's paradise. Complete with a small apple orchard, rhododendron sanctuary, succulent slope, vegetable garden, woodland walk, grape vines, various rare citrus trees, and my personal favorite, the BERRIES! Mostly raspberries, but true to their collector's nature, they couldn't stop at just one variety...however, whatever those varieties were, they are a mystery to all of us now.

When it came time to clean out the property after grandma's passing, the family came from far and wide to take turns gawking and helping. I always knew grandma and grandpa liked to keep things, but I don't think I quite grasped the magnitude until we began opening up closets, cabinets, drawers and files. We even found a bizarre stash of some rare, and not so rare coins above the sink in the kitchen, hidden away behind a ceiling tile...we were all about to learn a lot about our dearly departed.

Now, unearthing 5 decades of non-perishable treasures was one thing, but the freezers were on a whole different level of *"what kind of mental disorder is this?! And is it genetic?"* My mom had the task of cleaning out the scariest freezer; an upright unit where grandma kept berries in cardboard milk containers, each marked with her own secret code to remember the year & variety. I only wish she had used a legend, or put her secret code into one of her endless files. But no, we were left to play her guessing games, even after her departure.

When mom was about halfway through taking out all the containers of berries, she came face to face with a large bird wrapped in plastic! My Uncle Jeff & Aunt Kath who had traveled from Missouri to help out, immediately came to her aid. Jeff & Kath are both professors of biology, and experts on our grandparent's odd behavior, so maybe they could shed some light on this discovery. Jeff matter-of-factly explained how sometimes grandma would come across a "special" or "rare" specimen that had died naturally on her property, and if it was in good enough shape the carcass would be donated to a museum to be taxidermied and put on display. She was thoughtful of future generations that way.

Jeff also added that he's got several birds in *his* freezer right now, and is grateful for this reminder to actually bring them to his local museum. So apparently this *IS* a genetic disorder, and it extends *way* beyond the berries.

P.S.

After reading this to my little brother, he informed me that when they remodeled my bedroom to make it a dining room, the _did_ indeed find a mummified hamster in the walls. I think it might have been Rainbow, my first hamster who escaped and was never seen again.

P.P.S.

Mom has since caught yet another chipmunk in the house, and called to inform me that he suffered the same frozen state as his distant cousin.

P.P.P.S.

In late October 2021 I thought my 100 lb Bernese Mountain Dog Pepper was dying. On a Friday I called my dad to ask him to break out the backhoe dig a grave for her at our family property on Lake Davis. When Pepper miraculously bounced back on Saturday, I called yet again to let him know he could pause the project. Feeling the need to make a joke to keep from crying, told him; "Pepper isn't allowed to die in the winter now, since I don't have enough room in my freezer." To which he replied without any hesitation; "That's okay, I do!"

There was a freak storm the very next day, Pepper took a turn for the worst and passed away peacefully on her own. Mother and I loaded Pepper into the car and when I called to ask my father if he'd ignored my instructions, and dug her a grave in spite of the weather, he replied: "Nope, this just might have to be a freezer trip."

And it came to pass, that Pepper "wintered at Lake Davis with my father" before we could hold a proper memorial/FUNeral, and bury her in the ground on June 12th, 2022.

About the Author

You can get in touch with Jamie by writing to:
  Jamie Mayne
  P.O. Box 1010
  Tahoe City, CA 96145

Or you may Email her at:
  LifeGoneSideways@gmail.com

Jamie's buddy Kris Carpenter, who designed the cover of this book, can be reached at:
  KCarpenter3@gmail.com

Made in USA - North Chelmsford, MA
1359507_9781959555148
02.09.2023 1456